This book was conceived, edited and designed by

McRae Publishing Ltd, London

info@mcraebooks.com
www.mcraepublishing.co.uk
Publishers Anne McRae, Marco Nardi

Project Director Anne McRae
Art Director Marco Nardi
Photography Brent Parker Jones
Text Carla Bardi
Editing Karin Bellford
Food Styling Lee Blaylock
Food Preparation Lute Clarke, Pierrick Boyer
Layouts Aurora Granata
Prepress Filippo Delle Monache

NOTE TO OUR READERS
Eating eggs or egg whites that are not completely cooked poses the possibility of salmonella food poisoning. The risk is greater for pregnant women, the elderly, the very young, and persons with impaired immune systems. If you are concerned about salmonella, you can use reconstituted powdered egg whites or pasteurized eggs.

ISBN 978-88-6098-330-5

Printed in China

CARLA BARDI

BAKING

200 COMFORTING RECIPES

contents

Colorful icons throughout the book provide extra information on the recipes, or hints and tips for cooking and serving.

1
hazelnut cookies

2
walnut & raisin cookies

3
chewy oat & raisin cookies

4
linzer squares

5
almond bars

6
coconut fudge brownies

7
strawberry muffins

8
banana muffins with chocolate chips

9
date & walnut muffins

10
quick apple tart

11
caramelized pastry with strawberries & cream

12
cranberry pinwheels

13
plum tart

14
apple & pineapple strudel

simple recipes

15
quick chocolate fudge cake

16
easy frosted lemon cake

17
quick glazed lime cake

18
cream cheese pound cake with raspberry coulis

19
cinnamon spice cake

20
light fruit cake

1 hazelnut cookies

- ½ cup (120 g) salted butter, softened
- ¾ cup (150 g) firmly packed dark brown sugar
- 1 large egg, lightly beaten
- ⅔ cup (100 g) all-purpose (plain) flour
- ½ cup (50 g) old-fashioned rolled oats
- 1½ tablespoons unsweetened cocoa powder
- ½ teaspoon baking powder
- 3½ ounces(100 g) white chocolate, coarsely chopped
- 3½ ounces (100 g) milk chocolate, coarsely chopped
- 1 cup (120 g) coarsely chopped hazelnuts

Preheat the oven to 350°F (180°C/gas 4). Butter a baking sheet. Beat the butter and brown sugar in a large bowl with an electric mixer on high speed until creamy. Add the egg, beating until just blended. Mix in the flour, oats, cocoa, and baking powder. Stir in both chocolates and the hazelnuts by hand.

Drop teaspoons of the mixture ½ inch (1 cm) apart on the prepared baking sheet. Bake for 10–15 minutes, until risen and craggy. Cool on the sheet for 2–3 minutes. Transfer to racks and let cool completely.

MAKES 16–20 • PREPARATION 15 MIN. • COOKING 10–15 MIN. • LEVEL 1

2 walnut & raisin cookies

- $3\frac{1}{4}$ cups (480 g) all-purpose (plain) flour
- $\frac{1}{2}$ teaspoon ground cinnamon
- 1 cup (250 g) salted butter, softened
- $1\frac{1}{2}$ cups (300 g) firmly packed light brown sugar
- 3 large eggs
- 1 teaspoon baking soda (bicarbonate of soda) dissolved in $1\frac{1}{2}$ tablespoons hot water
- 1 cup (100 g) coarsely chopped walnuts
- 1 cup (180 g) raisins

Preheat the oven to 350°F (180°C/gas 4). Butter three baking sheets. Mix the flour and cinnamon in a large bowl. Beat the butter and brown sugar in a large bowl with an electric mixer on high speed until creamy. Add the eggs one at a time, beating until just blended after each addition. Stir in the baking soda mixture. Mix in the dry ingredients, walnuts, and raisins by hand.

Drop tablespoons of dough 2 inches (5 cm) apart onto the prepared cookie sheets. Bake for 8–10 minutes, until just golden at the edges. Cool on the sheets for 2–3 minutes. Transfer to racks and let cool completely.

MAKES 45–50 • PREPARATION 15 MIN. • COOKING 8–10 MIN. • LEVEL 1

3 chewy oat & raisin cookies

- $\frac{2}{3}$ cup (100 g) whole-wheat (wholemeal) flour
- 1 teaspoon baking powder
- $\frac{2}{3}$ cup (100 g) old-fashioned rolled oats
- 3 tablespoons shredded (desiccated) coconut
- $\frac{1}{2}$ cup (60 g) shelled walnuts, coarsely chopped
- $\frac{1}{2}$ cup (90 g) golden raisins (sultanas)
- $\frac{1}{2}$ cup (120 g) salted butter, softened
- $\frac{1}{2}$ cup (100 g) firmly packed light brown sugar
- 1 large egg
- 1 large ripe banana, mashed
- 1 teaspoon vanilla extract (essence)
- $\frac{1}{2}$ teaspoon finely grated untreated orange zest

Preheat the oven to 350°F (180°C/gas 4). Butter two large baking sheets. Combine the flour, baking powder, rolled oats, coconut, walnuts, and golden raisins in a medium bowl.

Beat the butter and brown sugar in a medium bowl with an electric mixer on medium speed until creamy. Beat in the egg until just combined, followed by the banana, vanilla, and orange zest.

With the mixer on low speed, gradually beat in the flour and oat mixture until well blended.

Drop tablespoons of the dough onto the prepared baking sheets, spacing 2 inches (5-cm) apart. Bake for 12–15 minutes, until lightly browned.

Let the cookies cool on the baking sheet until they harden a little, 2–3 minutes. Transfer to racks and let cool completely.

MAKES 20–24 • PREPARATION 15 MIN. • COOKING 12–15 MIN. • LEVEL 1

These classic chewy cookies are perfect with a cup of tea or coffee. If you want them a little crisper, just bake 2–3 minutes longer.

4 linzer squares

- 2 cups (300 g) all-purpose (plain) flour
- 1/3 cup (50 g) ground rice
- 1 teaspoon ground cinnamon
- 1/2 teaspoon ground cloves
- 1/2 cup (100 g) sugar + extra to sprinkle
- 2/3 cup (150 g) cold salted butter, diced
- 1 tablespoon milk
- 1 cup (300 g) raspberry preserves (jam)

Preheat the oven to 400°F (200°C/gas 6). Line a 9-inch (23-cm) square baking pan with parchment paper. Combine the flour, ground rice, cinnamon, cloves, and sugar in a medium bowl. Cut or rub in the butter until fine crumbs form. Stir in the milk. Spoon three-quarters of the dough into the prepared pan, pressing down firmly to form an even layer.

Bake for 15–20 minutes, until firm and pale golden brown. Spread evenly with the raspberry preserves. Sprinkle with the remaining dough and extra sugar. Bake for 5–10 minutes, until the topping is golden. Cool completely in the pan.

MAKES 12–16 • PREPARATION 15 MIN. • COOKING 20–30 MIN. • LEVEL 1

5 almond bars

- $^1/_2$ cup (125 g) salted butter, softened
- $^1/_3$ cup (75 g) sugar + extra to sprinkle
- 1 small egg
- $^1/_2$ teaspoon almond extract (essence)
- $1^1/_3$ cups (200 g) all-purpose (plain) flour
- $^1/_2$ teaspoon ground cinnamon
- $^1/_2$ cup (75 g) flaked almonds

Preheat the oven to 350°F (180°C/gas 4). Butter an 8-inch (20-cm) square baking pan.

Beat the butter and sugar in a medium bowl with an electric mixer on medium speed until pale and creamy. Beat in the egg and almond extract. With the mixer on low speed, gradually beat in the flour and cinnamon. Spoon into the prepared pan, pressing into the corners. Sprinkle with the almonds and a little extra sugar.

Bake for 20–25 minutes, until pale golden brown. Cool completely in the pan.

MAKES 12–16 • PREPARATION 15 MIN. • COOKING 20–25 MIN. • LEVEL 1

6 coconut fudge brownies

- 2/3 cup (100 g) unsweetened cocoa powder
- 1 cup (250 g) salted butter
- 2 1/2 cups (500 g) superfine (caster) sugar
- 4 large eggs, beaten
- 2/3 cup (100 g) all-purpose (plain) flour
- 2/3 cup (100 g) shredded (desiccated) coconut
- Confectioners' (icing) sugar, to dust (optional)

Preheat the oven to 350°F (180°C/gas 4). Butter a 9-inch (23-cm) square pan and line with parchment paper.

Combine the cocoa, butter, and sugar in a large saucepan over low heat and gently melt, stirring so that the mixture does not stick or burn. Set aside to cool for 5 minutes.

Gradually stir in the eggs, followed by the flour and coconut. Spoon into the prepared pan. Bake for 40–45 minutes, until dry on top and set around the edges.

Cool completely in the pan on a wire rack. Cut into squares.

MAKES 12–16 • PREPARATION 15 MIN. • COOKING 40–45 MIN. • LEVEL 1

Quick and easy to make, these brownies have a rich chocolate flavor and a lovely chewy coconut texture.

7 strawberry muffins

- $1\frac{1}{2}$ cups (225 g) sliced fresh strawberries
- $\frac{1}{2}$ cup (100 g) sugar + extra to sprinkle
- $1\frac{1}{4}$ cups (180 g) all-purpose (plain) flour
- $\frac{1}{2}$ cup (75 g) whole-wheat (wholemeal) flour
- 2 teaspoons baking powder
- $\frac{1}{2}$ teaspoon baking soda (bicarbonate of soda)
- $\frac{1}{2}$ teaspoon salt
- $\frac{1}{2}$ teaspoon ground cinnamon
- 1 cup (250 ml) milk
- $\frac{1}{4}$ cup (60 ml) vegetable oil
- 1 large egg
- 1 teaspoon vanilla extract (essence)

Preheat the oven to 400°F (200°C/gas 6). Line a standard 12-cup muffin tin with paper liners. Mash the strawberries and sugar in a bowl with a fork.

Mix both flours, baking powder, baking soda, salt, and cinnamon in a bowl. Whisk the milk, oil, egg, and vanilla in another bowl. Pour the milk and strawberry mixtures into the flour and stir until combined. Divide the batter evenly among the muffin cups. Sprinkle with sugar.

Bake for 15–20 minutes, until springy to the touch. Cool for 5 minutes in the pan, then transfer to a wire rack and let cool completely.

MAKES 12 • PREPARATION 15 MIN. • COOKING 15–20 MIN. • LEVEL 1

8 banana muffins
with chocolate chips

- 1 cup (150 g) whole-wheat (wholemeal) flour
- 1 cup (150 g) all-purpose (plain) flour
- 2 teaspoons baking powder
- 1/2 teaspoon baking soda (bicarbonate of soda)
- 1/2 cup (120 g) salted butter, softened
- 1 cup (200 g) sugar
- 3 large eggs
- 2 large very ripe bananas, mashed
- 1/4 cup (60 ml) milk
- 1 cup (180 g) dark chocolate chips
- 1 cup (120 g) walnuts, chopped

Preheat the oven to 375°F (190°C/gas 5). Arrange 20 foil baking cups on baking sheets. Mix both flours, baking powder, and baking soda in a large bowl. Beat the butter and sugar in a large bowl with an electric mixer on medium speed until pale and creamy. Add the eggs one at a time, beating until just blended after each addition. With the mixer on low, beat in the bananas, flour mixture, and milk. Stir in the chocolate chips and walnuts by hand. Divide the batter evenly among the foil cups.

Bake for 20–30 minutes, until a toothpick inserted into the center comes out clean. Cool the muffins on racks.

MAKES 20 • PREPARATION 15 MIN. • COOKING 20–30 MIN. • LEVEL 1

9 date & walnut muffins

- $3/4$ cup (120 g) whole-wheat (wholemeal) flour
- $3/4$ cup (120 g) all-purpose (plain) flour
- $1/3$ cup (75 g) firmly packed light brown sugar
- $1\frac{1}{2}$ teaspoons pumpkin-pie spice (allspice)
- 1 teaspoon baking soda (bicarbonate of soda)
- $1/2$ teaspoon salt
- $1/2$ cup (120 ml) milk
- $1/3$ cup (90 ml) molasses (treacle)
- 6 tablespoons (90 ml) light olive, canola, or safflower oil
- 2 large eggs
- $1\frac{1}{4}$ cups (150 g) walnuts, coarsely chopped
- 1 cup (180 g) pitted dates, coarsely chopped

Preheat the oven to 400°F (200°C/gas 6). Line a standard 12-cup muffin tin with paper liners. Combine both flours, brown sugar, pumpkin pie spice, baking soda, and salt in a large bowl.

Whisk the milk, molasses, oil, and eggs in a separate bowl. Stir into the dry ingredients, mixing until just combined. Stir in the walnuts and dates.

Divide the batter evenly among the muffin cups. Bake for 15–20 minutes, until a toothpick inserted into the center of a muffin comes out clean.

Cool in the pan for 5 minutes then turn out onto a wire rack and let cool completely.

MAKES 12 • PREPARATION 15 MIN. • COOKING 15–20 MIN. • LEVEL 1

If preparing these muffins for a special occasion, you can dress them up a little by wrapping them in pretty colored paper. Used scalloped scissors to make a decorative top edge and secure the paper with transparent scotch tape (sellotape).

10 quick apple tart

- 1 (8-ounce/250-g) sheet ready-rolled puff pastry
- 5 large eating apples, peeled, cored, and thinly sliced
- Freshly squeezed juice of 1 lemon
- 2 tablespoons salted butter, cut into small pieces
- 1 teaspoon vanilla extract (essence)
- 2 tablespoons sugar
- 3 heaped tablespoons apricot preserves (jam)
- 1 teaspoon cinnamon
- ½ cup (120 ml) lightly whipped heavy (double) cream

Preheat oven to 450°F (230°C/gas 8). Oil a 10-inch (25-cm) pie dish. Cut out a 12-inch (30-cm) circle of pastry and use it to line the base and ides of the pie dish. Toss the apples in the lemon juice and spread over the pastry. Dot with the butter, drizzle with the vanilla, and sprinkle with the sugar.

Bake for 15–20 minutes, until the apples are tender and the pastry is crisp. Warm the apricot preserves in a small saucepan and brush over the apples. Dust with the cinnamon and serve hot with a dollop of cream.

SERVES 6–8 • PREPARATION 15 MIN. • COOKING 15–20 MIN. • LEVEL 1

11 caramelized pastry
with strawberries & cream

- 2 (8-ounce/250-g) sheets ready-rolled puff pastry
- $\frac{1}{3}$ cup (50 g) confectioner's (icing) sugar
- 1 vanilla bean
- 1 cup (250 ml) heavy (double) cream
- $\frac{1}{4}$ cup (50 g) sugar
- 2 cups (300 g) fresh strawberries, quartered

Preheat the oven to 450°F (230°C/gas 8). Grease a large baking sheet. Put the pastry on the prepared baking sheet, place another baking sheet on top, and bake for 15–20 minutes, until golden. Preheat an overhead broiler (grill) to high. Dust the pastry with the confectioner's sugar and caramelize under the broiler, 3–5 minutes. Cut into 12 neat rectangles.

Split the vanilla bean and scrape the seeds into the cream. Beat with the sugar until thickened. Put a piece of pastry on each serving plate, top with a dollop of cream and some strawberries, and cover with another piece of pastry. Serve warm.

SERVES 6 • PREPARATION 15 MIN. • COOKING 18–25 MIN. • LEVEL 1

12 cranberry pinwheels

- ½ cup (100 g) sugar + extra to sprinkle
- 2 teaspoons ground cinnamon
- ½ teaspoon ground pumpkin pie spice (allspice)
- ½ teaspoon ground ginger
- ½ teaspoon ground nutmeg
- 2 (8-ounce/250-g) sheets ready-rolled puff pastry
- ¼ cup (60 g) butter, melted
- 2 cups (350 g) chopped candied (glacé) cranberries
- 1 large egg, beaten

Combine the sugar, cinnamon, pumpkin pie spice, ginger, and nutmeg in a small bowl.

Sprinkle a work surface generously with extra sugar. Place one puff pastry sheet on the sugared surface. Cut in half to form two even rectangles. Brush with melted butter, leaving a 1-inch (2.5-cm) border along one long side. Sprinkle each rectangle with 1½ tablespoons of spiced sugar and a quarter of the candied cranberries.

Brush the border with egg. Starting at the long side opposite the glazed border, tightly roll up each rectangle, pressing firmly to seal the edges.

Wrap each log separately in plastic wrap (cling film). Repeat with remaining pastry, butter, spiced sugar, candied fruit, and egg to create 2 more logs. Chill until firm, at least 3 hours and up to 1 day.

Preheat the oven to 400°F (200°C/gas 6). Line three baking sheets with parchment paper. Using a serrated knife, cut the logs into ½-inch (1-cm) thick rounds. Arrange on the prepared baking sheets, spacing 1 inch (2.5 cm) apart. Bake for 20–25 minutes, until golden brown. Cool on the baking sheets for 5 minutes. Transfer to wire racks and let cool completely.

MAKES 30–40 • PREPARATION 20 MIN. + 3–24 HR. TO CHILL • COOKING 20–25 MIN. • LEVEL 1

13 plum tart

- 1 (8-ounce/250-g) sheet ready-rolled puff pastry
- 2 pounds (1 kg) ripe red plums, pitted and quartered
- 3/4 cup (150 g) firmly packed light brown sugar
- 2 tablespoons finely ground almonds
- 1 teaspoon ground cinnamon
- 1/4 cup (30 g) walnuts, coarsely chopped
- 2 tablespoons salted butter, cubed
- 1 large egg, lightly beaten
- 2 tablespoons raw sugar
- 1 cup (250 ml) crème fraîche
- 3 tablespoons honey

Preheat the oven to 400°F (200°C/gas 6). Line a baking sheet with parchment paper. Cut out a 12-inch (30-cm) circle of pastry and place on the baking sheet. Mix the plums, brown sugar, almonds, cinnamon, and walnuts in a bowl. Spread on the pastry and top with the butter. Fold the edges of the pastry to make a border. Brush with the egg and sprinkle with the raw sugar.

Bake for 20 minutes. Decrease the oven temperature to 350°F (180°C/gas 4) and bake for 25–30 more minutes, until golden brown and bubbling. Beat the crème fraîche and honey in a small bowl until combined. Serve warm with a dollop of honeyed crème fraîche.

SERVES 6–8 • PREPARATION 20 MIN. • COOKING 45–50 MIN. • LEVEL 1

14 apple & pineapple strudel

- 6 sheets filo (phyllo) pastry, thawed if frozen
- 2 tablespoons unsalted butter, melted
- 3 apples, peeled, cored, and thinly sliced
- 1 cup (250 g) crushed pineapple, drained
- 1 tablespoon cornstarch (cornflour)
- 2 teaspoons pumpkin pie spice (allspice)
- 1 teaspoon vanilla extract (essence)
- 3 tablespoons honey

Preheat the oven to 400°F (200°C/gas 6). Oil a large baking sheet. Lay the sheets of filo out flat and cover with parchment paper and a damp kitchen towel. Brush the first sheet with butter. Top with a second sheet and brush with butter. Repeat with three more sheets.

Mix the apples, pineapple, cornstarch, pumpkin pie spice, vanilla, and honey in a medium bowl. Spread the pastry with the pineapple mixture, leaving a 1-inch (2.5-cm) border all around. Cover with the remaining sheet of filo. Brush with butter. Carefully roll up the strudel. Transfer to the baking sheet. Bake for 20–30 minutes, until golden brown. Serve warm.

SERVES 6–8 • PREPARATION 15 MIN. • COOKING 20–30 MIN. • LEVEL 1

15 quick chocolate fudge cake

- 1 cup (150 g) all-purpose (plain) flour
- $\frac{1}{3}$ cup (50 g) unsweetened cocoa powder
- $\frac{1}{2}$ teaspoon baking soda (bicarbonate of soda)
- $\frac{1}{2}$ cup (120 g) salted butter, melted and warm
- $1\frac{1}{4}$ cups (250 g) firmly packed light brown sugar
- 2 large eggs
- 1 teaspoon vanilla extract (essence)
- $\frac{1}{2}$ cup (120 ml) hot water
- 1 recipe dark chocolate ganache (see page 152), optional

Preheat the oven to 350°F (180°C/gas 4). Butter a 9-inch (23-cm) square pan and line with parchment paper.

Combine the flour, cocoa, and baking soda in a bowl. Beat the melted butter and brown sugar with a wooden spoon in a large bowl. Add the eggs and vanilla and stir until well blended. Add the flour mixture all at once and stir until just combined. Pour the hot water over the batter and stir until just incorporated and smooth. Spoon the batter into the prepared pan.

Bake for 30 minutes, until a toothpick inserted into the center comes out clean. Let cool in the pan for 10 minutes. Turn out onto a wire rack and let cool completely.

If serving with the ganache, spread over the top and sides of the cooled cake and let set for at least one hour before serving.

SERVES 6–8 • PREPARATION 10–15 MIN. + 1 HR. TO SET (IF SERVING WITH GANACHE) • COOKING 30 MIN. • LEVEL 1

You can whip this cake up in just a few minutes. Serve it with coffee at breakfast or brunch as is, or add a layer of sinful chocolate ganache and enjoy it as a family dessert.

16 easy frosted lemon cake

Cake
- 1½ cups (225 g) all-purpose (plain) flour
- ¾ cup (150 g) sugar
- 3 large eggs
- ½ cup (120 g) salted butter, softened
- ⅓ cup (90 ml) milk
- 1 tablespoon finely grated untreated lemon zest
- 1½ teaspoons baking powder

Frosting
- 1½ cups (225 g) confectioners' (icing) sugar
- 2 tablespoons salted butter, melted
- 2 tablespoons freshly squeezed lemon juice
- 2 tablespoons shredded (desiccated) coconut

Cake Preheat the oven to 350°F (180°C/gas 4). Lightly grease a 9-inch (23-cm) square pan. Beat the flour, sugar, eggs, butter, milk, lemon zest, and baking powder in a large bowl with an electric mixer on low speed until well blended. Increase the mixer speed to medium and beat until pale and thick, 3–4 minutes. Spoon the batter into the prepared pan. Bake for 40–45 minutes, until a toothpick inserted into the center comes out clean. Cool completely in the pan on a rack.

Frosting Beat the confectioners' sugar and butter in a medium bowl, adding enough of the lemon juice to make a spreadable frosting. Spread the cake with the frosting and sprinkle with the coconut.

SERVES 6–8 • PREPARATION 20 MIN. • COOKING 40–45 MIN. • LEVEL 1

17 quick glazed lime cake

Cake

- $^{3}/_{4}$ cup (180 g) salted butter
- $1^{1}/_{2}$ cups (225 g) confectioners' (icing) sugar
- 2 large eggs
- $^{1}/_{4}$ cup (60 ml) milk
- $1^{1}/_{3}$ cups (200 g) all-purpose (plain) flour
- 2 teaspoons baking powder

Lime Glaze

- $^{1}/_{4}$ cup (60 ml) freshly squeezed lime juice
- 1 tablespoon finely grated lime zest
- $^{1}/_{4}$ cup (50 g) sugar
- 1 cup (150 g) confectioners' (icing) sugar

Cake Preheat the oven to 350°F (180°C/gas 4). Butter and flour an 8-inch (20-cm) springform pan. Beat the butter and confectioners' sugar in large bowl with an electric mixer on medium speed until pale and creamy. Add the eggs one at a time, bearing until just combined after each addition. With the mixer on low speed, gradually beat in the flour, baking powder, and milk. Spoon into the pan. Bake for 35–40 minutes, until a toothpick inserted into the center comes out clean.

Lime Glaze Mix the lime juice, zest, and sugar in small bowl. Using a skewer, poke holes all over the warm cake. Spoon half the lime syrup over the cake. Let cool. Whisk the confectioners' sugar into the remaining lime syrup. Drizzle over the cake and let cool completely.

SERVES 6–8 • PREPARATION 25 MIN. • COOKING 35–40 MIN. • LEVEL 1

18 cream cheese pound cake
with raspberry coulis

Cake
- 1 cup (250 g) salted butter, softened
- 8 ounces (250 g) cream cheese, at room temperature
- 3 cups (600 g) sugar
- 1 teaspoon salt
- 6 large eggs
- 4 teaspoons vanilla extract (essence)
- 3 cups (450 g) all-purpose (plain) flour
- 2 teaspoons baking powder

Raspberry Coulis
- 2 cups (300 g) fresh raspberries
- 2 teaspoons freshly squeezed lemon juice

Cake Lightly grease and flour an 11-inch (28-cm) tube pan. Beat the butter and cream cheese in large bowl with an electric mixer on medium speed until fluffy, 3–4 minutes. Add the sugar and beat until very pale and creamy, 8–10 minutes.

Add the eggs one at a time, beating until just blended after each addition. Beat in the vanilla. With the mixer on low speed, gradually beat in the flour and baking powder.

Spoon the batter into the prepared pan, smoothing the top with the back of the spoon.

Place the cake in a cold oven. Set the oven temperature at 250°F (130°C/gas ½) and bake for 30 minutes. Increase the oven temperature to 300°F (150°C/gas 2) and bake for about 1 hour, until a toothpick inserted into the center comes out clean.

Cool the cake in pan for 15 minutes. Turn out onto a wire rack and let cool completely.

Raspberry Coulis Mash the raspberries in a bowl with the lemon juice. Cut the cake into wedges and serve with a dollop of raspberry coulis.

SERVES 12–15 • PREPARATION 20 MIN. • COOKING 1½ HR. • LEVEL 1

19 cinnamon spice cake

Cake
- 2 cups (300 g) all-purpose (plain) flour
- ½ cup (100 g) firmly packed brown sugar
- 1 tablespoon baking powder
- ¼ cup (60 g) cold salted butter, cut up
- ½ cup (125 ml) milk
- 1 large egg, lightly beaten
- ½ cup (90 g) raisins

Topping
- ¼ cup (50 g) firmly packed brown sugar
- 1 teaspoon ground cinnamon
- 1 teaspoon pumpkin pie spice (allspice)
- 1 teaspoon ground ginger
- 3 tablespoons butter, melted

Cake Preheat the oven to 375°F (190°C/gas 5). Lightly grease and flour a 9-inch (23-cm) square baking pan.

Stir the flour, brown sugar, and baking powder in a large bowl. Use a pastry blender to cut in the butter until the mixture resembles fine crumbs. Stir in the milk and egg, then the raisins. The batter will be sticky and thick. Spoon into the prepared pan, spreading evenly.

Topping Mix the brown sugar, cinnamon, pumpkin pie spice, and ginger in a small bowl. Sprinkle over the batter. Drizzle with the butter. Bake for 30–40 minutes, until a toothpick inserted into the center comes out clean. Leave to cool in the pan for 10 minutes. Serve warm or at room temperature straight from the pan.

SERVES 6–8 • PREPARATION 15 MIN. • COOKING 30–40 MIN. • LEVEL 1

20 light fruit cake

- 2 cups (300 g) all-purpose (plain) flour
- 1 teaspoon baking powder
- 1 teaspoon ground nutmeg
- $^3/_4$ cup (180 g) salted butter, softened
- $^1/_2$ cup (100 g) sugar
- 3 large eggs
- $^1/_2$ cup (120 ml) milk
- 1 tablespoon sweet sherry
- 1 pound (500 g) candied (glacé) fruit, coarsely chopped
- $^1/_2$ cup (80 g) blanched almonds, coarsely chopped

Preheat the oven to 325°F (170°C/gas 3). Line an 8-inch (20-cm) square baking pan with parchment paper.

Combine the flour, baking powder, and nutmeg in a bowl. Beat the butter and sugar in a large bowl with an electric mixer on medium speed until pale and creamy. Add the eggs one at a time, beating until just blended after each addition. With the mixer on low speed, gradually beat in the flour mixture, alternating with the milk. Stir in the sherry, candied fruit, and almonds by hand. Spoon the batter into the prepared pan.

Bake for 2 hours, until a toothpick inserted into the center comes out clean. Cool in the pan for 10 minutes. Turn out onto a wire rack and let cool completely.

SERVES 8–12 • PREPARATION 30 MIN. • COOKING 2 HR. • LEVEL 2

caraway rose cookies

chocolate chip shortbread

thumbprint shortbread with strawberry jam

crisp walnut cookies

hazelnut meringues

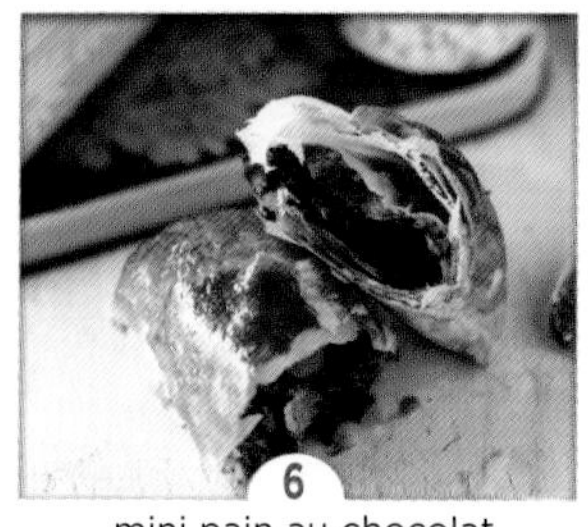

mini pain au chocolat

apple turnovers

puff pastry hearts & flowers

marbled meringues with berries & cream

cornflake squares

almond & coffee squares

12 gooey chocolate puddings

13 chocolate raspberry tart

14 orange tart

just a few ingredients

15 blueberry pie

16 orange syrup cake

17 almond cake

18 chocolate roulade

19 coffee vacherin

20 raspberry roulade

1 caraway rose cookies

- $1\frac{1}{2}$ cups (225 g) all-purpose (plain) flour
- 1 cup (200 g) sugar
- 1 teaspoon caraway seeds
- 1 large egg yolk + 3 large egg whites
- 1 tablespoon rose water

Mix the flour, sugar, and caraway seeds in a medium bowl. Beat in the egg yolk and egg whites and rose water to form a stiff dough. Press into a disk, wrap in plastic wrap (cling film), and chill for 30 minutes.

Preheat the oven to 325°F (170°C/gas 3). Butter two baking sheets. Roll out the dough on a floured surface to $\frac{1}{8}$-inch (3-mm) thick. Use a 2-inch (5-cm) cookie cutter to cut out cookies. Gather the dough scraps, re-roll, and continue cutting out until all the dough is used. Transfer to the baking sheets, spacing well. Bake until golden brown, 10–15 minutes. Cool on the sheets for 2–3 minutes. Transfer to racks to cool completely.

MAKES 25–30 • PREPARATION 20 MIN. + 30 MIN. TO CHILL • COOKING 10–15 MIN. • LEVEL 1

2 chocolate chip shortbread

- 2 cups (300 g) all-purpose (plain) flour
- ½ cup (75 g) confectioners' (icing) sugar
- 2 tablespoons cornstarch (cornflour)
- 1 cup (250 g) salted butter, cut up
- 2 cups (360 g) dark chocolate chips

Preheat the oven to 325°F (170°C/gas 3). Butter two 8-inch (20-cm) springform pans. Mix the flour, confectioners' sugar, and cornstarch in a large bowl. Use a pastry blender to cut in the butter until the mixture resembles coarse crumbs. Stir in the chocolate chips. Firmly press the mixture into the prepared pans to form smooth even layers.

Bake until golden, 15–20 minutes. Cool for 5 minutes in the pans. Loosen and remove the springform sides. Let cool completely. Cut each round into sixteen wedges.

MAKES 32 • PREPARATION 15 MIN. • COOKING 15–20 MIN. • LEVEL 1

3 thumbprint shortbread
with strawberry jam

- 1 cup (250 g) salted butter, softened
- 3/4 cup (150 g) sugar
- 1/2 teaspoon almond extract (essence)
- 1 2/3 cups (250 g) all-purpose (plain) flour
- 1/2 cup (150 g) seedless raspberry preserves (jam)

Preheat the oven to 350°F (180°C/gas 4). Line two large baking sheets with parchment paper. Beat the butter and sugar in a large bowl with an electric mixer on medium speed until pale and creamy. Beat in the almond extract.

With the mixer on low speed, beat in the flour until the dough just comes together. Roll pieces of dough into walnut-size balls. Place on the prepared baking sheets and flatten slightly, making a hollow in the center of each cookie with your thumb. Use a teaspoon to fill the hollows with raspberry preserves.

Bake for 15–18 minutes, until pale golden brown. Let the cookies cool on the baking sheets until they harden a little, 2–3 minutes. Transfer to racks and let cool completely.

MAKES 25–30 • PREPARATION 15 MIN. • COOKING 15–18 MIN. • LEVEL 1

You can vary these cookies by replacing the raspberry preserves with strawberry or apricot preserves.

4 crisp walnut cookies

- $2\frac{1}{3}$ cups (350 g) walnut halves
- $1\frac{1}{2}$ cups (250 g) sugar
- 3 large eggs
- Finely grated zest and juice of $\frac{1}{2}$ organic lemon

Preheat the oven to 325°F (170°C/gas 3). Line three baking sheets first with parchment paper and then with rice paper. Spread the walnuts on a baking sheet. Toast for 5–7 minutes, until golden brown. Chop in a food processor with $\frac{1}{4}$ cup (50 g) of sugar until finely ground.

Beat the eggs and the remaining 1 cup (200 g) of sugar in a large bowl with an electric mixer on high speed until pale and thick. Fold in the lemon zest and juice and ground walnut mixture.

Drop rounded teaspoons onto the prepared baking sheets, spacing $1\frac{1}{2}$ inches (4 cm) apart. Bake for 12–15 minutes, until lightly browned. Transfer the cookies still on the rice paper to racks to cool.

MAKES 35–40 • PREPARATION 20 MIN. • COOKING 12–15 MIN. • LEVEL 2

5 hazelnut meringues

- 2 cups (300 g) hazelnuts
- 1 cup (200 g) superfine (caster) sugar
- 4 large egg whites
- 1/4 teaspoon salt

Preheat the oven to 325°F (170°C/gas 3). Line two baking sheets with parchment paper. Spread the hazelnuts on a large baking sheet. Toast for 5–7 minutes, until golden brown. Chop in a food processor with 1/2 cup (100 g) of sugar until finely ground. Reduce the oven temperature to 250°F (130°C/gas 1/2).

Beat the egg whites and salt in a large bowl with an electric mixer on medium speed until soft peaks form. Beat in the remaining sugar until stiff glossy peaks form. Fold in the hazelnut mixture.

Drop teaspoons of the mixture 2 inches (5 cm) apart on the prepared baking sheets. Bake until dry and crisp, 25–35 minutes. Transfer while still on the parchment paper to wire racks to cool.

MAKES 30–35 • PREPARATION 20 MIN. • COOKING 25–35 MIN. • LEVEL 1

6 mini pain au chocolat

- 2 (8-ounce/250-g) sheets ready-rolled puff pastry
- 1 large egg
- 1 tablespoon water
- 14 ounces (400 g) dark chocolate, broken into small squares

Preheat the oven to 400°F (200°C/gas 6). Line two large baking sheets with parchment paper. Cut each piece of pastry into 12 even-size squares. Whisk the egg and water in a small bowl to make a glaze. Brush each pastry square with the glaze, using half the glaze.

Put 1–2 squares of chocolate on the edge of each pastry square. Roll up dough tightly, enclosing the chocolate. Place the pastry rolls on the baking sheets, seam-side down. Brush the tops of the pastry rolls with remaining egg glaze.

Bake for 12–15 minutes, until the pastries are golden brown. Serve warm or at room temperature.

MAKES 24 • PREPARATION 20 MIN. • COOKING 12–15 MIN. • LEVEL 2

If preferred, use milk or white chocolate instead of the dark chocolate. Or use a mixture of all three. The important thing is to choose a very good quality chocolate that will withstand the baking.

7 apple turnovers

- 1 (8-ounce/250-g) sheet ready-rolled puff pastry
- 1 apple, peeled, cored, and cut into quarters
- 1/2 cup (125 ml) hot water
- 1/4 cup (60 ml) light corn (golden) syrup

Preheat the oven to 400°F (200°C/gas 6). Cut the pastry into four even-size squares. Place an apple quarter in the center of each pastry square. Draw up the pastry edges and pinch them together to seal. Arrange the turnovers on a baking sheet. Bake for 15–20 minutes, until golden.

Mix the water and corn syrup and drizzle over the hot turnovers. Serve warm.

SERVES 4 • PREPARATION 10 MIN. • COOKING 15–20 MIN. • LEVEL 1

8 puff pastry hearts & flowers

- 2 (8-ounce/250-g) sheets ready-rolled puff pastry
- 1 cup (300 ml) raspberry preserves (jam)

Preheat the oven to 400°F (200°C/gas 6). Line a large baking sheet with parchment paper. Use heart- and flower-shaped cookie cutters to stamp out hearts and flowers from the pastry. Use the offcuts of pastry to make stems and leaves for the flowers. Spoon 1–2 teaspoons of preserves onto each heart and flower. Transfer to the prepared baking sheet, spacing well.

Bake for 10–12 minutes, until the pastry is crisp and golden. Let the pastries cool on the baking sheet for 10 minutes, then transfer to wire racks and let cool completely. Carefully lift the pastries off the parchment paper using a metal spatula.

SERVES 12 • PREPARATION 25 MIN. • COOKING 10–12 MIN. • LEVEL 1

9 marbled meringues
with berries & cream

- 3 large egg whites
- 3/4 cup (150 g) superfine (caster) sugar
- Few drops red food coloring
- 1/2 cup (120 ml) heavy (double) cream
- 2 cups (300 g) mixed summer berries

Preheat the oven to 300°F (150°C/gas 2). Line a large baking sheet with parchment paper.

Beat the egg whites in a medium bowl with an electric mixer on medium speed until frothy. Gradually beat in the sugar until thick and glossy. Spoon the mixture onto the prepared baking sheet in six even-size meringues, spacing well. Use the spoon to make an indent in the top of each meringue. Dip a toothpick into the red food coloring and swirl it in the top of the meringues to create a marbled effect.

Put the baking sheet in the oven. Decrease the oven temperature to 250°F (130°C/gas 1/2), and bake for 40–50 minutes, until dry. Turn off the oven and leave to dry out overnight.

Beat the cream until thick. Spoon into the hollows in the meringues just before serving and top with the berries.

MAKES 6 • PREPARATION 20 MIN. + 12 HR. TO COOL • COOKING 40–50 MIN. • LEVEL 2

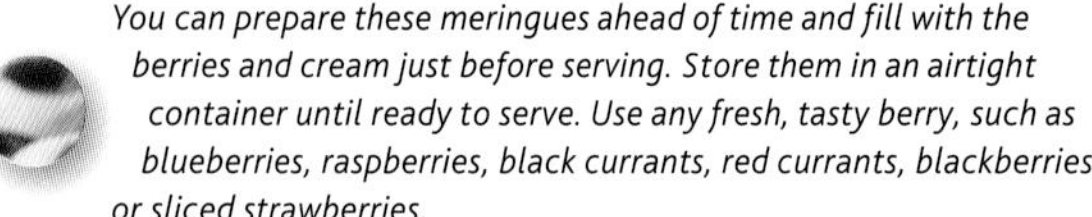

You can prepare these meringues ahead of time and fill with the berries and cream just before serving. Store them in an airtight container until ready to serve. Use any fresh, tasty berry, such as blueberries, raspberries, black currants, red currants, blackberries, or sliced strawberries.

10 cornflake squares

- $^{3}/_{4}$ cup (90 g) corn flakes
- $^{1}/_{2}$ cup (125 g) salted butter, melted
- $^{1}/_{2}$ cup (100 g) firmly packed dark brown sugar
- $^{1}/_{2}$ cup (50 g) candied green cherries
- $^{1}/_{2}$ teaspoon ground ginger

Preheat the oven to 350°F (180°C/gas 4). Butter an 8-inch (20-cm) square baking pan. Mix the corn flakes, butter, brown sugar, candied cherries, and ginger in a medium bowl. Firmly press the mixture into the pan.

Bake for 25–30 minutes, until golden brown. Let cool before cutting into squares.

MAKES 16 • PREPARATION 10 MIN. • COOKING 25–30 MIN. • LEVEL 1

11 almond & coffee squares

- 2 teaspoons instant coffee granules dissolved in 2 tablespoons of hot water
- $^{3}/_{4}$ cup (150 g) sugar
- $1^{1}/_{3}$ cups (200 g) coarsely chopped almonds
- 2 large egg whites
- Confectioners' (icing) sugar, to dust

Preheat the oven to 350°F (180°C/gas 4). Butter an 8-inch (20-cm) square baking pan. Stir the coffee mixture and sugar in a small saucepan over medium heat until the sugar is completely dissolved. Stir in the almonds. Remove from the heat.

Beat the egg whites in a large bowl with an electric mixer on high speed until stiff peaks form. Use a large rubber spatula to fold into the almond mixture. Spoon into the prepared pan. Bake for 35–40 minutes, until a toothpick inserted into the center comes out clean. Let cool completely before cutting into squares. Dust with the confectioners' sugar.

MAKES 16 • PREPARATION 15 MIN. • COOKING 35–40 MIN. • LEVEL 1

12 gooey chocolate puddings

- 8 tablespoons (120 g) salted butter, cut up
- $\frac{1}{2}$ cup (100 g) superfine (caster) sugar
- 4 ounces (125 g) dark chocolate, coarsely chopped
- 2 large eggs + 2 large egg yolks
- 2 teaspoons all-purpose (plain) flour

Preheat the oven to 400°F (200°C/gas 6). Grease four small ramekins with 1 tablespoon of butter and sprinkle with a little of the sugar, shaking out the excess.

Melt the chocolate and remaining 7 tablespoons of butter in a double boiler over barely simmering water. Set aside.

Beat the eggs, egg yolks, and remaining sugar in a large bowl with an electric mixer on high speed until pale and thick.

Use a large rubber spatula to fold the chocolate mixture and flour into the beaten eggs. Pour the mixture evenly into the prepared ramekins. Bake for 10–12 minutes, until set. Serve warm.

MAKES 4 • PREPARATION 15 MIN. • COOKING 10–12 MIN. • LEVEL 2

These delicious little puddings are as easy to make as they are delicious to eat. Whip them up for a family dessert or snack.

13 chocolate raspberry tart

Crust
- 1 recipe shortcrust pastry (see page 106)

Filling
- 12 ounces (350 g) dark chocolate
- 2 cups (500 ml) light (single) cream
- 4 large egg yolks
- 2 cups (300 g) fresh raspberries, mashed with a fork

Crust Prepare the pastry and pre-bake the crust following the instructions on page 106. Decrease the oven temperature to 300°F (150°C/gas 2).

Filling Melt the chocolate with the cream in a double boiler over barely simmering water. Transfer to a large bowl and let cool. With an electric mixer on high speed, beat in the egg yolks. Use a large rubber spatula to fold in the raspberries. Pour the filling into pastry crust. Bake for 25–30 minutes, until the filling has set. Let cool completely before serving.

SERVES 8–12 • PREPARATION 15 MIN. + TIME FOR THE CRUST • COOKING 25–30 MIN. • LEVEL 2

14 orange tart

Crust

- 1 recipe shortcrust pastry (see page 106)

Filling

- 4 large eggs
- 1 cup (200 g) superfine (caster) sugar
- 1 cup (250 ml) light (single) cream
- 2 untreated blood oranges

Crust Prepare the pastry and pre-bake the crust following the instructions on page 106. Decrease the oven temperature to 300°F (150°C/gas 2).

Filling Mix the eggs, sugar, and cream in a medium bowl. Remove the zest from one of the oranges and cut the flesh into thin slices. Squeeze the juice from the remaining orange. Stir the juice into the beaten egg mixture. Pour the mixture into the pastry crust and arrange the orange slices on top. Bake for 25–30 minutes, until the filling has set. Let cool completely before serving.

SERVES 6–8 • PREPARATION 15 MIN. + TIME FOR THE CRUST • COOKING 25–30 MIN. • LEVEL 2

15 blueberry pie

Crust
- $1\frac{1}{2}$ recipes shortcrust pastry (see page 106)

Filling
- 3 cups (600 g) fresh or frozen blueberries
- $\frac{1}{3}$ cup (50 g) finely ground almonds
- $\frac{1}{4}$ cup (50 g) sugar + extra to sprinkle
- 2 teaspoons finely grated untreated lemon zest

Crust Prepare the shortcrust pastry. Divide into two pieces, one slightly larger than the other. Wrap in plastic wrap (cling film) and refrigerate for 1 hour.

Roll out the larger piece of pastry on a lightly floured work surface to $\frac{1}{8}$ inch (3 mm) thick. Line the base and sides of a 9-inch (23-cm) pie pan with the pastry, pressing it firmly around the edges of the pan. Chill for 30 minutes.

Filling Preheat the oven to 400°F (200°C/gas 6). Combine the blueberries, ground almonds, sugar, and lemon zest in a medium bowl. Pour into the prepared pie pan.

Roll out the smaller piece of pastry into a 10-inch (25-cm) circle and use it to cover the pie. Press down with your fingers around the edges to seal. Cut off any excess pastry and sprinkle with extra sugar. Bake for 40 minutes, until the pastry is golden brown. Serve warm.

SERVES 6–8 • PREPARATION 30 MIN. + $1\frac{1}{2}$ HR. TO CHILL • COOKING 40 MIN. • LEVEL 2

You can vary this pie by replacing the blueberries with the same weight of blackberries or a mixture of blackberries and sliced apples.

16 orange syrup cake

Cake
- $1\frac{1}{4}$ cups (250 g) sugar
- 4 large eggs, separated
- 1 cup (150 g) all-purpose (plain) flour
- 2 teaspoons baking powder

Orange Syrup
- 1 cup (250 ml) freshly squeezed orange juice
- $\frac{1}{3}$ cup (90 ml) dry Marsala wine or sherry

Cake Preheat the oven to 350°F (180°C/gas 4). Butter a 9 x 5-inch (23 x 12-cm) loaf pan. Line with parchment paper. Beat the sugar and egg yolks in a large bowl with an electric mixer on high speed until pale and thick. With the mixer on low speed, beat in the flour and baking powder. Beat the egg whites in a large bowl until stiff peaks form. Fold into the batter. Spoon the batter into the prepared pan. Bake for 30–40 minutes, until a toothpick inserted into the center comes out clean. Cool in the pan for 10 minutes. Turn out onto a rack. Remove the paper and let cool completely.

Orange Syrup Mix the orange juice and Marsala in a bowl. Poke holes in the cake with a skewer and place on a rack over a large bowl or plate. Drizzle with the syrup.

SERVES 6–8 • PREPARATION 20 MIN. • COOKING 30–40 MIN. • LEVEL 1

17 almond cake

- 4 large eggs
- $1\frac{1}{3}$ cups (200 g) confectioners' (icing) sugar
- 1 teaspoon finely grated organic lemon zest
- 1 teaspoon ground cinnamon
- $1\frac{1}{3}$ cups (200 g) finely ground almonds

Preheat the oven to 325°F (170°C/gas 3). Butter a 9-inch (23-cm) springform pan. Beat the eggs, 1 cup (150 g) of confectioners' sugar, lemon zest, and cinnamon in a large bowl with an electric mixer on medium speed until thick and creamy. Fold in the almonds. Spoon the batter into the prepared pan, smoothing the surface with the back of the spoon. Bake for 30–35 minutes, until a toothpick inserted into the center comes out clean.

Cool in the pan for 10 minutes, then turn out onto a wire rack. Carefully remove the paper and let cool completely, at least one hour. Dust with the remaining confectioners' sugar just before serving.

SERVES 6–8 • PREPARATION 20 MIN. + 1 HR. TO COOL • COOKING 30–35 MIN. • LEVEL 1

18 chocolate roulade

- 8 ounces (250 g) dark chocolate, coarsely chopped
- 8 large eggs, separated
- $1^1/_4$ cups (250 g) sugar
- $^1/_4$ teaspoon salt
- 1 recipe chocolate frosting (see page 170)

Preheat the oven to 350°F (180°C/gas 4). Butter a 10 x 15-inch (25 x 35-cm) jelly-roll pan. Line with parchment paper. Melt the chocolate in a double boiler over barely simmering water. Let cool.

Beat the egg yolks and sugar in a large bowl with an electric mixer on medium speed until pale and thick. Gradually beat in the chocolate. Beat the egg whites and salt in a large bowl until stiff peaks form. Fold them into the chocolate mixture. Spoon the batter into the prepared pan.

Bake for 20 minutes, until springy to the touch. Cool the cake in the pan for 5 minutes. Dust a clean kitchen towel with sugar. Turn the cake out onto the towel. Carefully remove the parchment paper and trim the edges of the cake. Using the towel as a guide, roll the cake up.

Prepare the frosting and refrigerate for 30 minutes, until cooled and thickened. Unroll the cake and spread with half the frosting. Reroll the cake and spread with the remaining frosting.

SERVES 10–12 • PREPARATION 30 MIN. + 1 HR. TO COOL • COOKING 20 MIN. • LEVEL 3

This is a very rich chocolate roulade. Serve in thin slices for dessert. You can lighten it up a little with fresh raspberries or sliced strawberries. Because it contains no flour, it makes an ideal gluten-free dessert for those with gluten intolerance.

19 coffee vacherin

- 5 large egg whites
- $1\frac{1}{2}$ cups (300 g) sugar + 2 tablespoons extra
- 1 tablespoon coffee liqueur
- $1\frac{1}{2}$ cups (375 ml) heavy (double) cream
- Whole coffee beans, to decorate

Preheat the oven to 250°F (130°C/gas ½). Line a baking sheet with parchment paper and mark two 9-inch (23-cm) circles on the paper. Beat the egg whites in a large bowl with an electric mixer on medium speed until frothy. Beat in the sugar until stiff and glossy. Fold in the liqueur. Spoon into a pastry bag fitted with a ½-inch (1-cm) tip and pipe into two spiral disks on the paper. Bake for 1 hour, until crisp. Turn off the oven and leave the door ajar until cool, about 1 hour.

Beat the cream and extra sugar in a bowl until stiff. Place a layer of vacherin on a plate. Spread with three-quarters of the cream. Top with the remaining vacherin. Spoon the remaining cream into a pastry bag and decorate the top with rosettes. Top with coffee beans.

SERVES 6–8 • PREPARATION 30 MIN. + 1 HR. TO COOL • COOKING 1 HR. • LEVEL 2

20 raspberry roulade

- 6 large egg whites
- 1¼ cups (250 g) superfine (caster) sugar + extra to dust
- 2½ tablespoons cornstarch (cornflour)
- 1 cup (250 ml) heavy (double) cream
- 1 cup (150 g) fresh raspberries

Preheat the oven to 400°F (200°C/gas 6). Line a jelly-roll pan with parchment paper and lightly oil. Beat the egg whites in a bowl with an electric mixer on medium speed until frothy. Beat in the sugar until stiff and glossy. Fold in the cornstarch. Spread evenly in the prepared pan. Bake for 10 minutes. Remove from the oven and let cool for 30 minutes.

Beat the cream until thickened. Fold in the raspberries. Lay a kitchen towel on a work surface. Dust with extra sugar. Turn the meringue out onto the towel. Remove the paper. Spread with the filling. Roll up from a short side. Chill seam-side down for 2 hours.

SERVES 6–8 • PREPARATION 30 MIN. + 2½ HR. TO COOL & CHILL • COOKING 10 MIN. • LEVEL 3

1
crisp wheat germ cookies

2
coffee cookies
with hazelnuts

3
sunflower seed cookies
with brown sugar & oats

4
fruit & nut bars

5
seed & nut bars

6
brown sugar brownies
with peanuts & chocolate chips

7
apple muffins
with raisins & walnuts

8
apple & blueberry muffins
with crumble topping

9
raspberry muffins

10
frosted pineapple muffins

11
frosted carrot muffins

12
cinnamon spirals

13
cherry donuts

14
candied fruit buns

breakfast & brunch

15
danish breakfast rolls

16
streusel brunch cake

17
pear & pecan streusel cake

18
warm applesauce cake with walnut topping

19
pear & walnut cake

20
rhubarb & orange cake

1 crisp wheat germ cookies

- 3/4 cup (120 g) wheat germ, toasted
- 1/2 teaspoon baking soda (bicarbonate of soda)
- 1 teaspoon ground cinnamon
- 1/2 teaspoon ground nutmeg
- 1/2 cup (75 g) old-fashioned rolled oats
- 1/3 cup (70 g) sugar
- 1/3 cup (90 g) salted butter
- 1 tablespoon light corn (golden) syrup
- 1 tablespoon milk

Preheat the oven to 350°F (180°C/gas 4). Butter two large baking sheets. Stir the wheat germ, baking soda, cinnamon, and nutmeg in a large bowl. Stir in the oats and sugar. Melt the butter with the corn syrup and milk in a small saucepan over low heat. Pour into the dry ingredients and mix until smooth.

Form into balls the size of walnuts and place 2 inches (5 cm) apart on the prepared baking sheets, flattening slightly. Bake for 12–15 minutes, until golden brown. Cool the cookies completely on the baking sheets.

MAKES 24–28 • PREPARATION 15 MIN. • COOKING 12–15 MIN. • LEVEL 1

2 coffee cookies
with hazelnuts

- $1^1/_4$ cups (180 g) all-purpose (plain) flour
- 1 teaspoon baking powder
- $^1/_2$ cup (120 g) salted butter, softened
- $^3/_4$ cup (150 g) sugar
- 2 teaspoons instant coffee granules dissolved in 1 tablespoon boiling water
- 1 teaspoon vanilla extract (essence)
- $^1/_2$ cup (75 g) toasted hazelnuts

Preheat the oven to 325°F (170°C/gas 3). Butter two large baking sheets. Mix the flour and baking powder in a large bowl. Beat the butter and sugar in a large bowl with an electric mixer on medium speed until pale and creamy. Add the coffee mixture and vanilla. With the mixer on low speed, beat in the flour mixture.

Roll into balls the size of walnuts and place $1^1/_2$ inches (4 cm) apart on the prepared baking sheets, flattening slightly. Press three hazelnuts into the top of each cookie. Bake for 15–20 minutes, until firm to the touch. Let cool on the sheets for 2–3 minutes the transfer to wire racks and let cool completely.

MAKES 28–30 • PREPARATION 15 MIN. • COOKING 15–20 MIN. • LEVEL 1

3 sunflower seed cookies
with brown sugar & oats

- $1\frac{1}{2}$ cups (225 g) all-purpose (plain) flour
- 1 teaspoon baking soda (bicarbonate of soda)
- 1 cup (250 g) salted butter, softened
- 1 cup (200 g) firmly packed light brown sugar
- 1 cup (200 g) sugar
- $\frac{1}{2}$ teaspoon vanilla extract (essence)
- 2 large eggs
- 2 cups (300 g) old-fashioned rolled oats
- 1 cup (100 g) sunflower seeds

Preheat the oven to 350°F (180°C/gas 4). Butter three large baking sheets or line with parchment paper.

Combine the flour and baking soda in a medium bowl. Beat the butter, both sugars, and vanilla in a large bowl with an electric mixer on medium speed until creamy. Add the eggs one at a time, beating until just blended after each addition.

With the mixer on low speed, beat in the flour mixture, oats, and sunflower seeds.

Drop tablespoons of the dough 2 inches (5 cm) apart onto the prepared baking sheets.

Bake for 10–15 minutes, until golden brown. Let the cookies cool on the baking sheets until they harden a little, 2–3 minutes. Transfer to racks and let cool completely.

MAKES 35–40 • PREPARATION 20 MIN. • COOKING 10–15 MIN. • LEVEL 1

Packed with energy and goodness, these cookies are a healthy way to start the day. Sunflower seeds are a good source of dietary fiber, vitamin E, folate, magnesium, and selenium.

4 fruit & nut bars

- 1 cup (200 g) pitted dates
- $1\frac{1}{2}$ cups (225 g) old-fashioned oats
- 1 cup (150 g) pecans, toasted, finely chopped
- $\frac{1}{2}$ cup (60 g) macadamia nuts, coarsely chopped
- $\frac{1}{3}$ cup (60 g) dried papaya, coarsely chopped
- $\frac{1}{3}$ cup (60 g) dried cherries, coarsely chopped
- $\frac{1}{3}$ cup (60 g) dried blueberries
- 2 tablespoons oat bran
- 3 tablespoons ground flaxseed
- 2 tablespoons wheat germ
- $\frac{1}{2}$ teaspoon salt
- $\frac{1}{2}$ teaspoon ground cinnamon
- 3 tablespoons honey

Preheat the oven to 350°F (180°C/gas 4). Butter an 9-inch (23-cm) square baking pan.

Place the dates in a small saucepan, cover with cold water, and bring to a gentle simmer. Drain well and chop in a food processor until smooth. Combine the oats, pecans, macadamias, papaya, cherries, blueberries, oat bran, flaxseed, wheat germ, salt, and cinnamon in a large bowl. Mix in the dates and honey. Press the mixture into the prepared pan in an even layer.

Bake for 20–25 minutes, until firm and golden brown. Cool completely in the pan. Cut into bars.

MAKES 16–20 • PREPARATION 20 MIN. • COOKING 20–25 MIN. • LEVEL 1

5 seed & nut bars

- 1/3 cup (90 g) salted butter, softened
- 1/3 cup (90 ml) honey
- 1/2 cup (100 g) raw sugar (Demerara or Barbados)
- 1 1/2 cups (225 g) old-fashioned rolled oats
- 1/2 cup (60 g) coarsely chopped walnuts
- 1/2 cup (60 g) raisins
- 2 tablespoons pumpkin seeds
- 2 tablespoons sunflower seeds
- 2 tablespoons sesame seeds
- 2 tablespoons shredded (desiccated) coconut
- 1 teaspoon ground cinnamon

Preheat the oven to 375°F (190°C/gas 5). Butter a 7 x 11-inch (18 x 28-cm) baking pan. Stir the butter, honey, and raw sugar in a medium saucepan over low heat. Bring to a boil and simmer until the sugar has dissolved. Remove from the heat and stir in the oats, walnuts, raisins, pumpkin seeds, sunflower seeds, sesame seeds, coconut, and cinnamon. Spoon into the prepared pan.

Bake for 25–30 minutes, until just golden. Let cool completely in the pan before cutting into bars.

MAKES 16–20 • PREPARATION 15 MIN. • COOKING 25–30 MIN. • LEVEL 1

6 brown sugar brownies
with peanuts & chocolate chips

- 1 cup (150 g) all-purpose (plain) flour
- $1/4$ teaspoon baking soda (bicarbonate of soda)
- $1/2$ cup (120 g) salted butter
- $1\,1/4$ cups (250 g) dark brown sugar
- 2 large eggs
- 1 teaspoon vanilla extract (essence)
- $1/2$ cup salted roasted peanuts, divided
- $1/2$ cup (90 g) dark chocolate chips, divided

Preheat the oven to 350°F (180°C/gas 4). Butter and flour an 8-inch (20-cm) square baking pan. Combine the flour and baking soda in a medium bowl.

Melt the butter in a medium saucepan over low heat. Remove from the heat; add the brown sugar and whisk until smooth. Cool the mixture for 5 minutes then whisk in the eggs and vanilla.

Stir in the flour mixture followed by half of the peanuts and half the chocolate chips. Spread the batter evenly in the prepared pan. Sprinkle with the remaining peanuts and chocolate chips.

Bake for 30–35 minutes, until golden brown and a toothpick inserted into the center comes out clean. Cool in the pan on a wire rack.

Serve just barely warm or completely cool.

MAKES 12–16 • PREPARATION 20 MIN. • COOKING 30–35 MIN. • LEVEL 1

This is a rich brunch cake that is perfect for holidays, birthdays, and other special occasions. You can replace the peanuts with roasted pecans if preferred.

7 apple muffins
with raisins & walnuts

- $1\frac{1}{4}$ cups (300 ml) milk
- 1 cup (150 g) oat bran
- $\frac{1}{2}$ cup (75 g) whole-wheat (wholemeal) flour
- 1 cup (150 g) all-purpose (plain) flour
- 1 tablespoon baking powder
- 2 large eggs
- $\frac{1}{3}$ cup (90 g) salted butter, melted
- $\frac{1}{2}$ cup (100 g) firmly packed light brown sugar
- $\frac{1}{2}$ teaspoon vanilla extract (essence)
- 2 Granny Smith apples, peeled, cored, and chopped
- 2 tablespoons raisins
- $\frac{1}{4}$ cup (40 g) walnuts, toasted and chopped

Preheat the oven to 400°F (200°C/gas 6). Line a standard 12-cup muffin tin with paper liners. Put the milk and oat bran in a bowl. Combine both flours and the baking powder in a bowl. Whisk the eggs, butter, sugar, and vanilla in a medium bowl.

Stir the bran mixture into the egg mixture, then stir this mixture into the dry ingredients. Stir in the apples, raisins, and walnuts. Spoon into the muffin cups. Bake for 20–25 minutes, until golden brown. Turn the muffins out onto wire racks. Serve warm.

SERVES 4 • PREPARATION 15 MIN. • COOKING 20–25 MIN. • LEVEL 1

8 apple & blueberry muffins
with crumble topping

Crumble Topping
- 2 tablespoons salted butter
- 4 tablespoons all-purpose (plain) flour
- 2 tablespoons raw sugar

Muffins
- 2 cups (300 g) all-purpose (plain) flour
- 1 tablespoon baking powder
- 1 cup (200 g) sugar
- $^3/_4$ cup (180 ml) milk
- 1 large egg, beaten
- $^1/_2$ cup (120 g) salted butter, melted
- Finely grated zest of 1 untreated lemon
- 1 large apple, grated
- 1 cup (150 g) fresh blueberries
- $^1/_4$ cup (40 g) coarsely chopped pecans

Crumble Topping Rub the butter into the flour until it resembles fine bread crumbs. Stir in the sugar and work the mixture with your fingers until it forms nuggets.

Muffins Preheat the oven to 400°F (200°C/gas 6). Line a standard 12-cup muffin tin with paper liners. Mix the flour, baking powder, and sugar in a bowl. Whisk the milk, egg, butter, and lemon zest in another bowl. Stir the milk mixture into the flour mixture until combined. Stir in the apple, blueberries, and pecans. Spoon into the muffin cups and sprinkle with the crumble topping. Bake for 20–25 minutes, until risen and golden. Cool the muffins on racks for 5 minutes. Serve warm.

MAKES 12 • PREPARATION 15 MIN. • COOKING 20–25 MIN. • LEVEL 1

9 raspberry muffins

- 1 cup (150 g) all-purpose (plain) flour
- $1\frac{1}{2}$ teaspoons baking powder
- $\frac{1}{2}$ teaspoon baking soda (bicarbonate of soda)
- 1 teaspoon ground cinnamon
- $\frac{2}{3}$ cup (150 g) low-fat plain yogurt
- $\frac{1}{2}$ cup (100 g) firmly packed light brown sugar
- 1 large egg
- 2 tablespoons sunflower oil
- 1 teaspoon vanilla extract (essence)
- 1 cup (150 g) fresh or frozen raspberries, thawed if frozen
- 3–4 tablespoons raw sugar

Preheat the oven to 400°F (200°C/gas 6). Line a standard 12-cup muffin tin with paper liners.

Combine the flour, baking powder, baking soda, and cinnamon in a bowl. Whisk the yogurt, brown sugar, egg, sunflower oil, and vanilla in another bowl. Pour the yogurt mixture into the flour mixture and stir until just combined. Stir in the raspberries.

Spoon the batter into the muffin cups. Sprinkle each muffin with some raw sugar. Bake for 15–20 minutes, until risen and springy to the touch.

Turn the muffins out onto wire racks. Serve warm.

MAKES 12 • PREPARATION 15 MIN. • COOKING 15–20 MIN. • LEVEL 1

You can vary these muffins by replacing the raspberries with the same quantity of blueberries or strawberries.

10 frosted pineapple muffins

Muffins
- 1 cup (150 g) all-purpose (plain) flour
- 2½ teaspoons baking powder
- ½ teaspoon baking soda
- 1 cup (150 g) old-fashioned rolled oats
- ⅓ cup (90 g) salted butter
- ½ cup (100 g) sugar
- ½ teaspoon vanilla extract
- 1 large egg
- ½ cup (100 g) crushed pineapple, drained
- ¾ cup (180 ml) milk

Cream Cheese Frosting
- 8 ounces (250 g) cream cheese, softened
- 1 cup (150 g) confectioners' (icing) sugar
- 2 tablespoons freshly squeezed orange juice

Muffins Preheat the oven to 350°F (180°C/gas 4). Line a standard 12-cup muffin tin with paper liners. Mix the flour, baking powder, baking soda, and oats in a bowl. Beat the butter, sugar, and vanilla in a bowl with an electric mixer at medium speed until creamy. Add the egg, beating until just blended. With the mixer on low speed, gradually beat in the flour mixture, pineapple, and milk.

Spoon into the muffin cups. Bake for 20–25 minutes, until a toothpick inserted into a center comes out clean. Cool the muffins completely on wire racks.

Cream Cheese Frosting Beat the cream cheese, confectioners' sugar, and orange juice in a medium bowl until creamy. Spread on the muffins.

MAKES 12 • PREPARATION 20 MIN. • COOKING 20–25 MIN. • LEVEL 1

11 frosted carrot muffins

Muffins
- 2 cups (300 g) all-purpose (plain) flour
- $^{1}/_{2}$ cup (75 g) whole-wheat (wholemeal) flour
- 1 tablespoon baking powder
- $^{3}/_{4}$ cup (150 g) firmly packed brown sugar
- $^{1}/_{2}$ cup (120 g) salted butter, melted
- 2 large eggs, lightly beaten
- $1^{1}/_{2}$ cups (200 g) firmly packed finely grated carrots
- $^{1}/_{2}$ cup (120 ml) milk
- $^{1}/_{4}$ cup (60 ml) freshly squeezed lemon juice

Lemon Frosting
- 8 ounces (250 g) cream cheese, softened
- 1 cup (150 g) confectioners' (icing) sugar
- 1 tablespoon finely grated untreated lemon zest

Muffins Preheat the oven to 350°F (180°C/gas 4). Line a standard 12-cup muffin tin with paper liners. Combine both flours, baking powder, and brown sugar in a large bowl. Stir in the butter, eggs, carrots, milk, and lemon juice. Spoon into the muffin cups. Bake for 20–25 minutes, until golden brown. Cool the muffins completely on wire racks.

Lemon Frosting Beat the cream cheese, confectioners' sugar, and lemon zest in a medium bowl until creamy. Spread on the muffins.

MAKES 12 • PREPARATION 20 MIN. • COOKING 20–25 MIN. • LEVEL 1

12 cinnamon spirals

Dough
- 1/2 ounce (15 g) compressed fresh yeast or 1 (1/4-ounce/7-g) package active dry yeast
- 1/2 cup (120 ml) lukewarm milk
- 2 2/3 cups (400 g) all-purpose (plain) flour
- 1/4 cup (50 g) superfine (caster) sugar
- 1/3 cup (90 g) salted butter, melted
- 2 large egg yolks, lightly beaten

Filling
- 1/2 cup (100 g) superfine (caster) sugar
- 1 tablespoon ground cinnamon
- 1/3 cup (90 g) butter, melted

Dough Mix the yeast and milk in a small bowl. Set aside until frothy, 5–10 minutes. Combine the flour and sugar in a large bowl. Add the yeast mixture, butter, and egg yolks and mix well. Transfer to a floured work surface and knead until smooth and elastic, about 10 minutes. Form into a ball, place in an oiled bowl, and cover with a clean kitchen towel. Let rise in a warm place until doubled in bulk, 60–90 minutes.

Line two large baking sheets with parchment paper. Punch the risen dough down, and knead for 1 minute. Divide the dough in two and roll into 15 x 12-inch (37 x 30 cm) rectangles, about 1/4 inch (5 mm) thick.

Filling Combine the sugar and cinnamon in a small bowl, mixing well. Brush the dough with half the melted butter and sprinkle each rectangle with one-third of the cinnamon sugar. Roll up one long side of the dough to the center, then roll up the other side, so that they meet in the middle. Press the edges together to join. Cut into 1-inch (2.5-cm) thick slices. Sprinkle with the remaining cinnamon sugar. Place on the baking sheets, sugar-side up. Let rise in a warm place for 30 minutes.

Preheat the oven to 375°F (190°C/gas 5). Brush the spirals with the remaining butter. Bake for 15–20 minutes, until golden brown. Transfer to a rack to cool.

MAKES 20–24 • PREPARATION 1 HR. + 1 1/2–2 HR. TO RISE
COOKING 15–20 MIN. • LEVEL 2

13 cherry donuts

- 1 ounce (30 g) compressed fresh yeast or 2 ($1/4$-ounce/ 7-g) packages active dry yeast
- 1 cup (250 ml) lukewarm milk
- $4\frac{1}{3}$ cups (650 g) all-purpose (plain) flour
- $3/4$ cup (150 g) sugar
- 2 large eggs
- $1/2$ cup (120 g) salted butter, softened
- $1/2$ cup (150 g) cherry preserves (jelly)
- 4 cups (1 liter) vegetable oil, to fry
- Confectioners' sugar, to dust

Stir the yeast and milk in a small bowl. Set aside until frothy, 5–10 minutes. Stir the flour, yeast mixture, sugar, and eggs in a bowl. Transfer to a floured surface and knead until smooth and elastic, about 10 minutes. Knead the butter into the dough. Set aside to rest until doubled in bulk, about 1 hour. Roll the dough out on a floured work surface to $1/2$ inch (1 cm) thick. Use 3-inch (7.5-cm) pastry cutters to cut out disks. Brush half the disks with the jelly. Place the remaining halves on top and seal the edges.

Heat the oil in a deep-fryer. Test the oil temperature by adding a small piece of bread. If the bread bubbles to the surface and turns golden, the oil is ready. Fry the donuts in batches until golden brown. Drain on paper towels. Dust with confectioners' sugar and serve hot.

MAKES 12–16 • PREPARATION 40 MIN. + 1 HR. TO RISE • COOKING 45 MIN. • LEVEL 3

14 candied fruit buns

- $\frac{1}{2}$ ounce (15 g) compressed fresh yeast or 1 ($\frac{1}{4}$-ounce/7-g) package active dry yeast
- $\frac{3}{4}$ cup (180 ml) lukewarm water
- $\frac{1}{4}$ cup (50 g) sugar
- 2 cups (300 g) all-purpose (plain) flour
- $\frac{1}{4}$ teaspoon salt
- 2 tablespoons vegetable oil
- $\frac{1}{2}$ cup (90 g) golden raisins (sultanas)
- 3 tablespoons pine nuts
- 2 tablespoons chopped mixed candied (glacé) orange and lemon peel

Oil a large baking sheet. Stir the yeast, $\frac{1}{4}$ cup (60 ml) of water, and 1 teaspoon sugar in a bowl. Set aside until frothy, 5–10 minutes. Combine the flour and salt in a large bowl. Stir in the yeast mixture, remaining $\frac{1}{2}$ cup (120 ml) of water, sugar, and oil. Cover and let rise in a warm place until doubled in bulk, about 2 hours.

Transfer to a floured work surface. Knead in the golden raisins, pine nuts, and candied peel. Bring together then divide into 12 smooth balls. Arrange the balls, well spaced, on the prepared baking sheet. Cover with a kitchen towel and let rise until doubled in bulk, about 1 hour. Preheat the oven to 375°F (190°C/gas 5). Bake for 15–20 minutes, until golden. Transfer to racks to cool.

MAKES 12 • PREPARATION 30 MIN. + 3 HR. TO RISE • COOKING 15–20 MIN. • LEVEL 2

15 danish breakfast rolls

- 2 tablespoons fine dry bread crumbs
- ½ ounce (15 g) compressed fresh yeast or 1 (¼-ounce/7-g) package active dry yeast
- ½ cup (120 ml) lukewarm milk
- ½ cup (100 g) sugar
- 1⅔ cups (250 g) all-purpose (plain) flour
- ½ teaspoon vanilla extract (essence)
- ¼ teaspoon salt
- 4 large egg yolks + 1 large egg, lightly beaten
- ½ cup (120 g) salted butter, melted
- 1 cup (180 g) golden raisins (sultanas)

Preheat the oven to 350°F (180°C gas 4). Butter a 10-inch (26-cm) springform pan. Sprinkle with the bread crumbs. Stir the yeast, milk, and 1 teaspoon sugar in a small bowl. Set aside until frothy, 5–10 minutes. Combine the flour, 1 tablespoon sugar, vanilla, and salt in a large bowl. Add the egg yolks. Stir in the yeast mixture until a smooth dough is formed.

Transfer to a lightly floured work surface and knead by hand until smooth and elastic, about 10 minutes. Break off a piece slightly larger than an egg and knead for a few seconds. Knead the remaining dough for a few seconds. Shape each piece of dough into a ball and place in two separate bowls. Cover with kitchen towels and let rise until doubled in bulk, about 30 minutes.

Roll out the smaller dough ball on a floured surface to ⅛ inch (3 mm) thick. Fit into the base of the prepared pan. Roll out the larger dough ball into a 16 x 7-inch (40 x 18-cm) rectangle. Brush with the melted butter and sprinkle with the remaining sugar and raisins. From a long side, roll up the dough jelly-roll fashion. Cut into 1½-inch (4-cm) thick slices. Arrange evenly on the dough base. Cover and let rest until the slices have expanded to fill the pan, about 1 hour. Brush with the egg. Bake for 30–35 minutes, until golden brown. Cool the cake in the pan for 10 minutes. Serve warm.

SERVES 6–8 • PREPARATION 30 MIN. + 1½ HR. TO RISE • COOKING 30–35 MIN. • LEVEL 2

16 streusel brunch cake

Topping
- $^{1}/_{3}$ cup (70 g) brown sugar
- $^{1}/_{3}$ cup (70 g) brown sugar
- 1 teaspoon ground cinnamon
- $^{1}/_{3}$ cup (90 g) salted butter, melted
- $^{1}/_{2}$ cup (75 g) all-purpose (plain) flour

Cake
- $2^{1}/_{2}$ cups (375 g) all-purpose (plain) flour
- 1 teaspoon baking soda (bicarbonate of soda)
- $^{3}/_{4}$ teaspoon baking powder
- $^{3}/_{4}$ cup (180 g) salted butter
- $1^{1}/_{2}$ cups (300 g) sugar
- 2 large eggs
- $1^{1}/_{3}$ cups (300 ml) sour cream
- 1 teaspoon vanilla extract (essence)

Topping Mix both sugars and cinnamon in a medium bowl. Stir in the warm melted butter. Add the flour and stir until clumpy.

Cake Preheat the oven to 350°F (180°C/gas 4). Butter a 9 x 13-inch (23 x 33-cm) baking pan. Combine the flour, baking soda, and baking powder in a bowl. Beat the butter and sugar until pale and creamy. Add the eggs one at a time, beating until just blended after each addition. With the mixer on low speed, beat in the sour cream, vanilla extract, and flour mixture. Spoon the batter into the baking pan. Sprinkle with the topping.

Bake for about 50 minutes, until a toothpick inserted into the center comes out clean. Serve warm.

SERVES 8–10 • PREPARATION 20 MIN. • COOKING 50 MIN. • LEVEL 1

17 pear & pecan streusel cake

Topping
- $1\frac{1}{2}$ cups (180 g) pecans
- $\frac{1}{3}$ cup (70 g) brown sugar
- 2 tablespoons all-purpose (plain) flour
- 1 teaspoon ground cinnamon
- 2 tablespoons salted butter

Cake
- 3 cups (450 g) all-purpose (plain) flour
- 2 teaspoons baking powder
- $\frac{1}{2}$ teaspoon baking soda (bicarbonate of soda)
- 1 cup (250 g) salted butter
- 1 cup (200 g) sugar
- $\frac{3}{4}$ cup (150 g) firmly packed brown sugar
- 3 large eggs
- 1 teaspoon finely grated untreated lemon zest
- 1 teaspoon vanilla extract
- $\frac{1}{2}$ cup (120 ml) sour cream
- $\frac{1}{2}$ cup (120 ml) milk
- 1 large pear, peeled, cored, and thinly sliced

Topping Blend the pecans, brown sugar, flour, and cinnamon in a food processor until the nuts are coarsely chopped. Add the butter and blend until clumpy.

Cake Preheat the oven to 350°F (180°C/gas 4). Butter a 9 x 13-inch (23 x 33-cm) baking pan. Combine the flour, baking powder, and baking soda in a bowl. Beat the butter and both sugars until creamy. Beat in the eggs one at a time. With the mixer on low speed, beat in the lemon zest and vanilla, alternating with the sour cream, milk, and flour mixture. Spread half the batter in the pan. Sprinkle with half the topping and cover with the pear. Cover with the remaining batter and topping. Bake for 50 minutes, until golden brown. Serve warm.

SERVES 8–10 • PREPARATION 20 MIN. • COOKING 50 MIN. • LEVEL 1

18 warm applesauce cake
with walnut topping

Applesauce Cake
- 2 cups (300 g) all-purpose (plain) flour
- 1 teaspoon baking powder
- 1 teaspoon baking soda (bicarbonate of soda)
- 3/4 teaspoon ground cinnamon
- 1/3 cup (90 g) salted butter, softened
- 1 1/4 cups (250 g) sugar
- 2 large eggs
- 3/4 cup (180 g) smooth homemade or store-bought applesauce
- 1 cup (250 ml) sour cream

Walnut Topping
- 1/2 cup (120 g) salted butter
- 1/2 cup (100 g) firmly packed light brown sugar
- 1/2 cup (100 g) sugar
- 2 teaspoons ground cinnamon
- 1 cup (150 g) all-purpose (plain) flour
- 1/4 cup (30 g) confectioners' (icing) sugar
- 1 cup (120 g) whole walnuts, coarsely chopped

Applesauce Cake Preheat the oven to 350°F (180°C/gas 4). Butter a 9-inch (23-cm) baking pan. Line with parchment paper. Combine the flour, baking powder, baking soda, and cinnamon in a bowl.

Beat the butter and sugar in a large bowl with an electric mixer on medium speed until pale and creamy. Add the eggs one at a time, beating until just combined. With the mixer on low speed, beat in the flour mixture, applesauce, and sour cream. Spoon the batter into the prepared pan.

Bake for 15 minutes, until the edges of the cake are slightly set and the rest is very jiggly.

Walnut Topping Prepare the topping while the cake is in the oven. Melt the butter over low heat. Add both sugars and the cinnamon and stir until blended. Add the flour, confectioners' sugar, and walnuts, mixing with your fingers until crumbly and clumping together.

Scatter evenly over the half-baked cake. Bake for 30–35 minutes more, until golden brown and a toothpick inserted in the center comes out clean. Let cool on a rack for 15 minutes. Serve warm.

SERVES 8–10 • PREPARATION 20 MIN. • COOKING 45–50 MIN.
LEVEL 1

19 pear & walnut cake

- 2 cups (300 g) all-purpose (plain) flour
- 1 teaspoon baking powder
- 1 teaspoon ground ginger
- ½ cup (120 g) salted butter, softened
- ¾ cup (100 g) firmly packed brown sugar
- 2 large eggs
- ½ cup (120 ml) milk
- 1 teaspoon baking soda (bicarbonate of soda)
- ¼ cup (30 g) candied (glacé) ginger, chopped
- ⅓ cup (50 g) walnuts, coarsely chopped
- 2 medium pears, peeled, cored, and thinly sliced

Preheat the oven to 350°F (180°C/gas 4). Grease a 9-inch (23-cm) square cake pan. Combine the flour, baking powder, and ginger in a bowl. Beat the butter and sugar in a medium bowl with an electric mixer on medium speed until creamy. Add the eggs one at a time, beating until just blended after each addition.

Combine the milk and baking soda in a small bowl. With the mixer on low speed, beat the flour mixture, milk, candied ginger, and walnuts into the batter. Spoon into the prepared pan and cover with the pears.

Bake for 40–45 minutes, until golden brown and firm to the touch. Leave to cool in the pan for 10 minutes. Turn out onto a wire rack. Serve warm.

SERVES 8–10 • PREPARATION 20 MIN. • COOKING 40–50. • LEVEL 1

20 rhubarb & orange cake

- 2 cups (300 g) all-purpose (plain) flour
- 2 teaspoons baking powder
- 1/2 cup (120 g) salted butter, softened
- 1 cup (200 g) sugar
- 2 teaspoons finely grated untreated orange zest
- 1 teaspoon vanilla extract (essence)
- 2 large eggs
- 1/2 cup (120 ml) milk
- 1/2 teaspoon baking soda (bicarbonate of soda)
- 2 cups (300 g) rhubarb, thinly sliced
- Confectioners' (icing) sugar, to dust

Preheat the oven to 325°F (170°C/gas 3). Grease a 9-inch (23-cm) springform pan. Combine the flour and baking powder in a medium bowl. Beat the butter, sugar, orange zest, and vanilla with an electric mixer on medium speed until pale and creamy. Add the eggs one at a time, beating until just blended after each addition.

Combine the milk and baking soda in a small bowl. With the mixer on low speed, beat the milk and flour mixture into the batter. Spoon into the prepared pan and sprinkle the rhubarb over the top.

Bake for 45–50 minutes, until golden brown. Let cool in the pan for 10 minutes. Turn out onto a wire rack. Dust with confectioners' sugar. Serve warm .

SERVES 8–10 • PREPARATION 20 MIN. • COOKING 45–50. • LEVEL 1

1
oatmeal & raisin cookies

2
chocolate chip cookies

3
pinwheel cookies

4
bran muffins

5
fairy cakes

6
blueberry muffins

7
chocolate caramel squares

8
chocolate mint squares

9
chocolate walnut brownies

10
lemon macaroons

11
raspberry macaroons

12
lemon tart

13
pear & almond tart

14
raspberry bakewell tart

classics

15
white chocolate napoleon

16
tarte tatin

17
linzertorte

18
red velvet cake

19
chocolate mud cake

20
frosted carrot cake

1 oatmeal & raisin cookies

- $1\frac{1}{2}$ cups (225 g) all-purpose (plain) flour
- 1 cup (125 g) unsweetened shredded (desiccated) coconut

1 teaspoon baking soda (bicarbonate of soda)

- $\frac{1}{2}$ teaspoon ground cinnamon
- $\frac{1}{2}$ teaspoon ground ginger
- 1 cup (250 g) salted butter, softened
- 1 cup (200 g) firmly packed light brown sugar
- $\frac{1}{3}$ cup (90 ml) pure maple syrup
- 1 large egg
- $1\frac{1}{2}$ teaspoons vanilla extract (essence)
- 3 cups (375 g) old-fashioned rolled oats
- 1 cup (180 g) raisins

Preheat the oven to 325°F (170°C/gas 3). Line three baking sheets with parchment paper. Mix the flour, coconut, baking soda, cinnamon, and ginger in a bowl.

Beat the butter and brown sugar in a bowl with an electric mixer on medium speed until creamy. Add the maple syrup and beat until combined. Beat in the egg and vanilla. With the mixer on low speed, beat in the flour mixture, followed by the oats and raisins. Shape the dough into balls the size of walnuts. Place on the prepared cookie sheets, spacing 1 inch (2.5 cm) apart.

Bake for 15–20 minutes, until golden brown. Let cool on the sheets for 2–3 minutes. Transfer to racks to cool.

MAKES 30–35 • PREPARATION 15 MIN. • COOKING 15–20 MIN. • LEVEL 1

2 chocolate chip cookies

- $1\frac{2}{3}$ cups (250 g) all-purpose (plain) flour
- $\frac{1}{2}$ teaspoon baking soda (bicarbonate of soda)
- $\frac{3}{4}$ cup (180 g) salted butter, softened
- 1 cup (200 g) firmly packed dark brown sugar
- $\frac{1}{2}$ cup (100 g) sugar
- 1 large egg + 1 large egg yolk
- 1 tablespoon vanilla extract (essence)
- 2 cups (350 g) dark chocolate chips

Preheat the oven to 325°F (170°C/gas 3). Butter two large baking sheets. Combine the flour and baking soda in a medium bowl. Beat the butter and both sugars in a large bowl with an electric mixer on medium speed until creamy. Beat in the egg, egg yolk, and vanilla until just combined. With the mixer on low speed, beat in the flour mixture. Stir in the chocolate chips by hand.

Drop tablespoons of the dough onto the prepared baking sheets, leaving a 2-inch (5-cm) space between each one. Bake for 12–15 minutes, until the edges are lightly golden. Let the cookies cool on the baking sheets until they harden a little, 2–3 minutes. Transfer to racks and let cool completely.

MAKES 20–30 • PREPARATION 15 MIN. • COOKING 12–15 MIN. • LEVEL 1

3 pinwheel cookies

- $^3/_4$ cup (200 g) salted butter, softened
- $^3/_4$ cup (150 g) sugar
- 2 teaspoons vanilla extract (essence)
- 1 large egg
- 2 cups (300 g) all-purpose (plain) flour
- $^1/_4$ cup (30 g) unsweetened cocoa powder

Beat the butter and sugar in a large bowl with an electric mixer on medium speed until pale and creamy. Beat in the vanilla and egg.

With the mixer on low speed, gradually beat in the flour. Divide the dough into two equal portions. Beat the cocoa into one of the portions. Shape both portions into oblongs. Wrap in plastic wrap (cling film) and chill for 30 minutes.

Roll both pieces of dough into $^1/_4$-inch (5-mm) thick rectangles. Put the chocolate dough on top of the pale dough and trim the edges to neaten. Roll up lengthwise like a jelly roll. Wrap in plastic wrap and chill for 30 minutes.

Preheat the oven to 350°F (180°C/gas 4). Butter three large baking sheets or line with parchment paper.

Slice the dough into disks as thinly as you can. Place on the cookie sheets, spacing well. Bake for 12–15 minutes, until golden brown. Let cool on the baking sheets until they harden a little, 2–3 minutes. Transfer to racks and let cool completely.

MAKES 35–40 • PREPARATION 30 MIN. + 1 HR. TO CHILL • COOKING 12–15 MIN. • LEVEL 2

4 bran muffins

- $1\frac{1}{2}$ cups (150 g) bran
- 1 cup (150 g) all-purpose (plain) flour
- 1 teaspoon baking powder
- $\frac{1}{4}$ cup (50 g) firmly packed dark brown sugar
- $\frac{1}{4}$ cup (45 g) raisins
- $\frac{1}{4}$ teaspoon salt
- 1 tablespoon light corn (golden) syrup
- 1 tablespoon salted butter
- 1 cup (250 ml) milk
- 1 teaspoon baking soda (bicarbonate of soda)
- 1 large egg, lightly beaten
- 2 firm-ripe bananas, $1\frac{1}{2}$ mashed, $\frac{1}{2}$ thinly sliced
- 2 tablespoons raw sugar

Preheat the oven to 350°F (180°C/gas 4). Line a standard 12-cup muffin tin with paper liners. Combine the bran, flour, baking powder, brown sugar, raisins, and salt in a large bowl. Melt the corn syrup and butter in a small saucepan over low heat. Mix the milk and baking soda in a small bowl. Mix the corn syrup mixture, milk mixture, and egg into the dry ingredients until just blended. Stir in the mashed bananas.

Spoon the batter into the prepared muffin cups. Place a slice of banana on top of each muffin and sprinkle with the raw sugar. Bake for 25–30 minutes, until golden brown. Let cool in the pans for 5 minutes. Turn out onto racks. Serve warm or at room temperature.

MAKES 12 • PREPARATION 15 MIN. • COOKING 25–30 MIN. • LEVEL 1

5 fairy cakes

- 2 cups (300 g) all-purpose (plain) flour
- 2 teaspoons baking powder
- 2/3 cup (150 g) salted butter, softened
- 3/4 cup (150 g) sugar
- 1 teaspoon vanilla extract (essence)
- 2 large eggs
- 1/2 cup (120 ml) milk
- 1 tablespoon freshly squeezed lemon juice
- 1 cup (250 ml) heavy (double) cream
- 1/2 cup (150 g) strawberry preserves (jam)
- Confectioners' (icing) sugar, to dust

Preheat the oven to 350°F (180°C/gas 4). Arrange 20 foil baking cups on baking sheets. Mix the flour and baking powder in a bowl. Beat the butter, sugar, and vanilla in a bowl with an electric mixer at medium speed until pale and creamy. Add the eggs one at a time, beating until just blended after each addition. With the mixer on low speed, add the flour mixture, milk, and lemon juice. Spoon into the baking cups. Bake for 20–25 minutes, until golden brown. Cool on racks.

Beat the cream in a bowl until stiff. Cut a small circle about 1/2 inch (1 cm) deep in the top of each cake. Fill with 1 teaspoon of preserves and 2–3 teaspoons of cream. Dust the tops with confectioners' sugar. Cut them in half and arrange on the cakes like fairy wings.

MAKES 20 • PREPARATION 25 MIN. • COOKING 20–25 MIN. • LEVEL 1

6 blueberry muffins

- $3\frac{1}{3}$ cups (500 g) all-purpose (plain) flour
- $1\frac{1}{4}$ cups (250 g) sugar
- 1 tablespoon baking powder
- $\frac{1}{4}$ teaspoon baking soda (bicarbonate of soda)
- $\frac{1}{3}$ cup (90 g) salted butter, melted
- $\frac{1}{4}$ cup (60 ml) canola oil
- 2 large eggs
- 1 cup (250 ml) low-fat yogurt
- 1 cup (250 ml) whole milk
- 1 teaspoon vanilla extract (essence)
- 1 teaspoon finely grated untreated lemon zest
- $1\frac{1}{2}$ cups (250 g) fresh or frozen blueberries, thawed if frozen

Preheat the oven to 350°F (180°C/gas 4). Line two standard 12-cup muffin tins with paper liners.

Combine the flour, sugar, baking powder, and baking soda in a large bowl. Whisk the butter and oil in a medium bowl. Add the eggs, whisking to blend. Whisk in the yogurt, milk, vanilla, and lemon zest. Stir the yogurt mixture into the dry ingredients. Stir in the blueberries. Spoon the batter into the muffin cups.

Bake for 20–25 minutes, until a toothpick inserted into center comes out clean. Transfer the muffins to wire racks and let cool.

MAKES 24 • PREPARATION 15 MIN. • COOKING 20–25 MIN. • LEVEL 1

Serve these classic muffins warm at breakfast or brunch. If liked, you can frost them with a simple vanilla frosting (see our recipe on page 121) and serve with tea or coffee later in the day, or as a family dessert.

7 chocolate caramel squares

Caramel
- ½ cup (120 g) salted butter
- ½ cup (100 g) sugar
- 2 tablespoons light corn (golden) syrup
- 1 (14-ounce/400-ml) can sweetened condensed milk

Base
- ¾ cup (180 g) salted butter
- 5 tablespoons superfine (caster) sugar
- 1 teaspoon vanilla extract (essence)
- 1⅓ cups (200 g) all-purpose (plain) flour

Frosting
- 8 ounces (250 g) dark chocolate
- 1 tablespoon salted butter

Caramel Melt the butter with the sugar, corn syrup, and condensed milk in a saucepan over low heat. Bring to a boil, then simmer for 10 minutes. Let cool.

Base Preheat the oven to 350°F (180°C/gas 4). Grease a 9-inch (23-cm) square baking pan. Beat the butter, sugar, and vanilla with an electric mixer on medium speed until pale and creamy. With the mixer on low speed, beat in the flour. Press into the prepared pan. Bake for 20–25 minutes, until golden brown. Set aside on a wire rack to cool. Spread the caramel over the base. Chill until set, at least 1 hour.

Frosting Melt the chocolate and butter in a double boiler over barely simmering water. Spread over the caramel in an even layer. Let set, then cut into squares.

MAKES 16–20 • PREPARATION 30 MIN. + 1 HR. TO CHILL • COOKING 40–50 MIN. • LEVEL 3

8 chocolate mint squares

Base
- 2 ounces (60 g) dark chocolate, chopped
- $\frac{1}{2}$ cup (120 g) salted butter, softened
- 1 cup (200 g) sugar
- 2 large eggs, lightly beaten
- 1 teaspoon vanilla extract (essence)
- $\frac{1}{2}$ cup (75 g) all-purpose (plain) flour
- $\frac{1}{4}$ teaspoon ground cinnamon

Mint Cream
- 6 ounces (180 g) white chocolate, chopped
- 3 tablespoons heavy (double) cream
- $\frac{3}{4}$ teaspoon peppermint extract
- 1 recipe chocolate ganache (see page 130)

Base Preheat the oven to 350°F (180°C/gas 4). Grease a 9-inch (23-cm) square baking pan. Melt the chocolate in a double boiler over barely simmering water. Beat the butter and sugar with an electric mixer on medium speed until pale and creamy. Beat in the eggs, chocolate, and vanilla. With the mixer on low speed, beat in the flour and cinnamon. Spoon into the pan. Bake for 20–25 minutes, until firm. Cool on a rack for 30 minutes. Turn out onto the rack and let cool completely.

Mint Cream Melt the chocolate and cream in a double boiler over barely simmering water. Stir in peppermint extract. Spread over the base. Freeze for 30 minutes. Spread with the ganache. Let set then cut into squares.

MAKES 16–20 • PREPARATION 30 MIN. + 1 HR. TO COOL & FREEZE
COOKING 20–25 MIN. • LEVEL 2

9 chocolate walnut brownies

- $^2/_3$ cup (150 g) salted butter
- $1^1/_4$ cups (250 g) sugar
- 1 cup (150 g) unsweetened cocoa powder
- 2 teaspoons water
- 1 teaspoon vanilla extract (essence)
- 2 large eggs, chilled
- $^1/_3$ cup (50 g) all-purpose (plain) flour
- 1 cup (120 g) walnut pieces
- Confectioners' (icing) sugar, to dust

Preheat the oven to 350°F (180°C/gas 4). Line an 8-inch (20-cm) square baking pan with foil, leaving a 2-inch (5-cm) overhang. Butter the foil.

Melt the butter in a medium saucepan over medium-low heat. Simmer until the butter stops foaming and browned bits form at bottom of the pan, stirring often, about 5 minutes. Remove from the heat and add the sugar, cocoa, water, and vanilla. Stir to blend. Let cool for 5 minutes.

Add the eggs to the warm mixture one at a time, beating vigorously to blend after each addition. When the mixture looks thick and shiny, add the flour and stir until blended. Beat vigorously for 1 minute. Stir in the walnuts. Spoon the batter into the prepared pan.

Bake for 20–25 minutes, until a toothpick inserted into center comes out with just a few moist crumbs attached. Cool in the pan on a wire rack. Using the foil overhang, lift the brownies from the pan. Dust with confectioners' sugar and cut into squares.

MAKES 16 • PREPARATION 15 MIN. • COOKING 20–25 MIN. • LEVEL 1

This is another old favorite. If you like a gooey brownie, bake for a minute or two less than the times given here.

10 lemon macaroons

Macaroons
- $1\frac{1}{3}$ cups (200 g) confectioners' (icing) sugar
- 1 cup (150 g) ground almonds
- 3 large egg whites
- Pinch of salt
- $\frac{1}{3}$ cup (75 g) superfine (caster) sugar
- $\frac{1}{2}$ teaspoon lemon extract (essence)
- Few drops yellow food coloring

Filling
- $\frac{2}{3}$ cup (150 g) butter, softened
- $\frac{1}{2}$ cup (75 g) confectioners' (icing) sugar
- $\frac{1}{2}$ teaspoon lemon extract (essence)
- Few drops yellow food coloring

Macaroons Line three baking sheets with parchment paper. Chop the confectioners' sugar and almonds very finely in a food processor, then sift into a bowl. Beat the egg whites and salt in a medium bowl with an electric mixer on medium speed until frothy. Gradually beat in the sugar until thick and glossy. Fold in the lemon extract, food coloring, and almond mixture. Transfer to a piping bag and pipe out 36 small circles on the baking sheets, spacing well. Let rest for 30 minutes.

Preheat the oven to 350°F (180°C/gas 4). Bake the macaroons for 15–20 minutes, until risen and smooth on top. Let cool completely on the baking sheets.

Filling Beat the butter, confectioners' sugar, lemon extract, and food coloring until smooth. Sandwich the macaroons together with this mixture.

MAKES 18 • PREPARATION 45 MIN. + 30 MIN. TO REST • COOKING 15–20 MIN. • LEVEL 3

11 raspberry macaroons

Macaroons
- 4 large egg whites
- 2 cups (300 g) confectioners' (icing) sugar
- Few drops red food coloring
- 1 cup (150 g) finely ground almonds

Filling
- 1/2 cup (120 g) mascarpone cheese
- 1/2 cup (150 g) seedless raspberry preserves (jam)

Macaroons Line three baking sheets with parchment paper. Beat the egg whites in a large bowl with an electric mixer on medium speed until frothy. Gradually beat in the confectioners' sugar until thick and glossy. Add the food coloring and beat until pink, with no streaks. Use a large metal spoon to fold in the almonds.

Transfer to a piping bag and pipe out 40 circles about 2 inches (5 cm) in diameter on the baking sheets, spacing 1 inch (2.5 cm) apart. Let rest for 30 minutes.

Preheat the oven to 350°F (180°C/gas 4). Bake the macaroons for 20–25 minutes, until risen and smooth on top. Let cool completely on the baking sheets.

Filling Whisk the mascarpone and raspberry preserves in a small bowl. Sandwich the macaroons together.

MAKES 20 • PREPARATION 30 MIN. + 30 MIN. TO REST • COOKING 20–25 MIN. • LEVEL 3

12 lemon tart

Shortcrust Pastry
- $1^1/_3$ cups (200 g) all-purpose (plain) flour
- 1 tablespoon sugar
- $^1/_4$ teaspoon salt
- $^1/_3$ cup (90 g) unsalted butter, chilled and cut into $^1/_2$-inch (1-cm) cubes
- 3 tablespoons (or more) iced water

Filling
- $^1/_2$ cup (100 g) sugar
- 2 large eggs + 2 large egg yolks
- 1 tablespoon finely grated untreated lemon zest
- $^1/_3$ cup (90 ml) freshly squeezed lemon juice
- $^3/_4$ cup (180 ml) heavy (double) cream
- Confectioners' (icing) sugar, to dust

Shortcrust Pastry Blend the flour, sugar, and salt in a food processor for 5 seconds. Add the butter and blend until a very coarse meal forms. Add the iced water. Blend until moist clumps form, adding more iced water if necessary. Gather into a ball and flatten into a disk. Wrap in plastic wrap (cling film) and chill for 1 hour.

Preheat the oven to 375°F (190°C/gas 5). Roll out the dough on a floured work surface into a 12 inch (30 cm) round. Ease into a 9-inch (23-cm) tart pan with a removable bottom. Freeze until firm, about 10 minutes. Line the pastry with foil and dried beans or pie weights. Bake until just set, 15–20 minutes. Remove the foil and beans. Continue to bake until pale gold, piercing with a fork if it bubbles, about 10 minutes. Cool on a rack. Reduce the oven temperature to 350°F (180°C/gas 4).

Filling Whisk the sugar, eggs, egg yolks, and lemon zest and juice and in a saucepan. Whisk over medium-low heat until thickened and just beginning to bubble, about 5 minutes. Transfer to a medium bowl. Cool to just warm, stirring occasionally, about 15 minutes. Gradually whisk in the cream. Pour into the crust.

Bake until set in center and starting to puff at the edges, about 20 minutes. Cool in the pan on a rack. Chill for 2 hours. Dust with confectioners' sugar and serve.

SERVE 6–8 • PREPARATION 45 MIN. + 3 HR. TO COOL & CHILL
COOKING 60–65 MIN. • LEVEL 2

13 pear & almond tart

Crust
- 1 recipe shortcrust pastry (see page 106)

Filling
- 2/3 cup (80 g) blanched slivered almonds
- 1 tablespoon all-purpose (plain) flour
- 7 tablespoons sugar
- 1/3 cup (90 g) butter, softened
- 1 large egg
- 6 canned pear halves, drained and sliced
- Confectioners' (icing) sugar to dust

Crust Prepare the pastry and pre-bake the crust following the instructions on page 106.

Filling Preheat the oven to 350°F (180°C/gas 4). Finely grind the almonds and flour in a food processor. Mix in the sugar, and then the butter, blending until smooth. Mix in the egg. Transfer to a medium bowl. Cover and chill for 3 hours.

Spread the almond filling evenly in the crust. Arrange the pears on the filling. Bake for 45–50 minutes, until golden and a toothpick inserted into the center comes out clean. Cool in the pan on a wire rack. Dust with confectioners' sugar and serve.

SERVE 6–8 • PREPARATION 30 MIN. + 3 HR. TO CHILL & TIME FOR THE CRUST • COOKING 45–50 MIN. • LEVEL 2

14 raspberry bakewell tart

Crust

- 1 recipe shortcrust pastry (see page 106)

Filling

- 3/4 cup (250 g) raspberry preserves (jam)
- 1/2 vanilla bean, split lengthwise
- 1/2 cup (100 g) sugar
- 1/2 cup (120 g) unsalted butter, melted and cooled
- 4 large egg yolks + 3 large egg whites
- 1/4 teaspoon almond extract
- Pinch of salt
- 1 cup (120 g) roasted salted almonds

Crust Prepare the pastry and pre-bake the crust following the instructions on page 106.

Filling Preheat the oven to 350°F (180°C/gas 4). Spread the raspberry preserves evenly over the crust. Scrape the seeds from the vanilla bean into a medium bowl. Stir in the sugar. Add the butter, egg yolks, egg whites, almond extract, and salt and whisk to blend. Finely grind the almonds in a food processor. Stir into the filling, then pour into the crust.

Bake for 30–35 minutes, until browned on top and set in the center. Serve warm.

SERVE 6–8 • PREPARATION 45 MIN. + TIME FOR THE CRUST • COOKING 30–35 MIN. • LEVEL 2

15 white chocolate napoleon

Pastry
- 3 (8-ounce/250-g) sheets ready-rolled puff pastry
- 3 tablespoons confectioners' (icing) sugar

Vanilla Pastry Cream
- 5 large egg yolks
- 3/4 cup (150 g) sugar
- 1/3 cup (50 g) all-purpose (plain) flour
- 3 cups (750 ml) milk
- 1/8 teaspoon salt
- 1 teaspoon vanilla extract (essence)
- 1/2 cup (120 ml) heavy (double) cream

Frosting
- 8 ounces (250 g) white chocolate, coarsely chopped
- 1 ounce (30 g) dark chocolate, coarsely chopped

Pastry Preheat the oven to 400°F (200°C/gas 6). Line two baking sheets with parchment paper. Place the pastry on the sheets and prick all over with a fork. Bake for 15–20 minutes, until risen and golden brown. Sprinkle each sheet with 1 tablespoon of confectioners' sugar and return to the oven for 5 minutes to caramelize. Cool the pastry on wire racks.

Vanilla Pastry Cream Beat the egg yolks and sugar in a bowl with an electric mixer on high speed until pale and thick. Beat in the flour. Bring the milk to a boil with the salt and vanilla, then stir it into the egg mixture. Simmer over low heat, stirring constantly, until the mixture thickens, 5 minutes. Remove from the heat and let cool, about 1 hour. Beat the cream until stiff. Fold into the cooled pastry cream.

Place one pastry layer on a serving plate and spread with half the pastry cream. Cover with another pastry layer and cover with the remaining pastry cream. Top with the remaining layer of pastry.

Frosting Melt the white chocolate in a double boiler over barely simmering water. Spread over the cake. Melt the dark chocolate in a double boiler over barely simmering water. Spoon into a pastry bag. Pipe lines of dark chocolate into the white chocolate and draw a knife through the lines to create a pattern.

SERVES 8–12 • PREPARATION 1 HR. + 1 HR. TO COOL • COOKING 25–30 MIN. • LEVEL 3

16 tarte tatin

- 1 recipe shortcrust pastry (see page 106)
- $\frac{1}{2}$ cup (100 g) sugar
- 1 tablespoon cold water
- $1\frac{1}{4}$ cups (250 g) firmly packed dark brown sugar
- $\frac{1}{2}$ cup (125 g) butter, cut up
- 6 apples, peeled, cored and quartered

Prepare the shortcrust pastry. Wrap in plastic wrap (cling film) and chill in the refrigerator. Preheat the oven to 350°F (180°C/gas 4). Heat the sugar and water in a small saucepan over low heat until caramelized. Spoon the caramel into a 9-inch (23-cm) round cake pan. Sprinkle with 1 tablespoon of brown sugar and dot with the butter. Arrange the apples in the prepared pan and sprinkle with the remaining brown sugar.

Roll the pastry out into a 9-inch (23-cm) round on a lightly floured surface. Cover the apples with the pastry, sealing the edges. Bake for 40–45 minutes, until golden brown. Invert onto a serving plate. Serve warm .

SERVES 6–8 • PREPARATION 25 MIN. • COOKING 40–45 MIN. • LEVEL 2

17 linzertorte

- 1 cup (150 g) blanched almonds
- ½ cup (60 g) toasted hazelnuts
- 1⅓ cups (200 g) all-purpose (plain) flour
- 1 teaspoon ground cinnamon
- ½ teaspoon baking powder
- ¾ cup (180 g) salted butter
- 1 cup (200 g) sugar
- 1 large egg yolk
- 1⅓ cups (350 g) raspberry preserves (jam)
- Confectioners' (icing) sugar to dust

Grease a 9-inch (23-cm) springform pan. Chop the hazelnuts and almonds in a food processor until finely ground. Mix the flour, cinnamon, and baking powder in a bowl. Beat the butter and sugar with an electric mixer on medium speed until pale and creamy. Beat in the egg yolk. With the mixer on low speed, beat in the nut and flour mixtures.

Divide the dough in half. Press one half into the base and sides of the prepared pan. Spread with the raspberry preserves. Roll the remaining dough into a 10-inch (26-cm) disk. Use a fluted pastry wheel to cut into strips. Place over the preserves in a lattice pattern. Freeze for 30 minutes. Preheat the oven to 350°F (180°C/gas 4). Bake for 35–40 minutes, until golden brown. Dust with confectioners' sugar and serve.

SERVES 8 • PREPARATION 30 MIN. + 30 MIN. TO FREEZE • COOKING 35–40 MIN. • LEVEL 2

18 red velvet cake

Cake
- 3 cups (450 g) all-purpose (plain) flour
- $\frac{1}{2}$ cup (75 g) unsweetened cocoa powder
- $1\frac{1}{2}$ teaspoons baking powder
- $1\frac{1}{2}$ teaspoons baking soda (bicarbonate of soda)
- 1 cup (250 g) salted butter, softened
- $2\frac{1}{4}$ cups (450 g) firmly packed light brown sugar
- 3 tablespoons red food coloring
- $2\frac{1}{2}$ teaspoons vanilla extract (essence)
- 3 large eggs
- $1\frac{3}{4}$ cups (430 ml) milk

Frosting
- $1\frac{1}{4}$ pounds (650 g) cream cheese, softened
- $1\frac{1}{4}$ cups (300 g) salted butter, softened
- 2 teaspoons vanilla extract (essence)
- 7 cups (1 kg) confectioners' sugar

Cake Preheat the oven to 350°F (180°C/gas 4). Grease two deep 9-inch (23-cm) cake pans. Add 2 tablespoons of flour to each pan and shake to coat the bottom and sides. Sift the flour with the cocoa, baking powder, and baking soda. Beat the butter with the brown sugar, food coloring, and vanilla in a large bowl with an electric mixer on medium speed until creamy. Add the eggs one at a time, beating until just combined after each addition. With the mixer on low speed, beat in the flour mixture and milk. Spoon the batter into the pans.

Bake for 40–45 minutes, until a toothpick inserted into the center comes out clean. Cool in the pan for 15 minutes. Turn out onto a rack and let cool completely

Frosting Beat the cream cheese, butter, and vanilla in a large bowl until pale and creamy. Gradually beat in the confectioners' sugar, until fluffy.

Slice the rounded tops off the cakes. Crumble the trimmings into a bow and set aside. Slice each cake in half horizontally. Place one layer on a serving plate. Spread with $\frac{3}{4}$ cup of frosting. Repeat with the remaining three layers of cake and frosting. Spread the remaining frosting around the sides of the cake. Gently press the reserved crumbs into the sides of the cake until evenly coated. Chill for 2 hours before serving.

SERVES 12–15 • PREPARATION 1 HR. + 2 HR. TO CHILL • COOKING 40–45 MIN. • LEVEL 3

19 chocolate mud cake

- 1 cup (250 ml) water
- 3/4 cup (150 g) sugar
- 2/3 cup (150 g) salted butter, diced
- 1 1/4 pounds (600 g) dark chocolate, chopped
- 6 large eggs
- 1 recipe chocolate ganache (see page 130)

Preheat the oven to 350°F (180°C/gas 4). Butter a 10-inch (25-cm) springform pan. Line with parchment paper. Wrap the outside of the pan in foil. Mix the water and sugar in small saucepan. Bring to a boil, stirring until the sugar dissolves. Simmer for 5 minutes.

Melt the butter in a large saucepan over low heat. Add the chocolate and whisk until smooth. Whisk the sugar syrup into the chocolate. Let cool slightly. Add the eggs to the chocolate mixture and whisk until well blended. Spoon the batter into the pan. Place the cake pan in a roasting pan. Add enough boiling water to come halfway up sides of the cake pan. Bake for 50 minutes, until set. Cool the cake completely in the pan. Spread with the ganache just before serving.

SERVES 12–15 • PREPARATION 20 MIN. • COOKING 55 MIN. • LEVEL 2

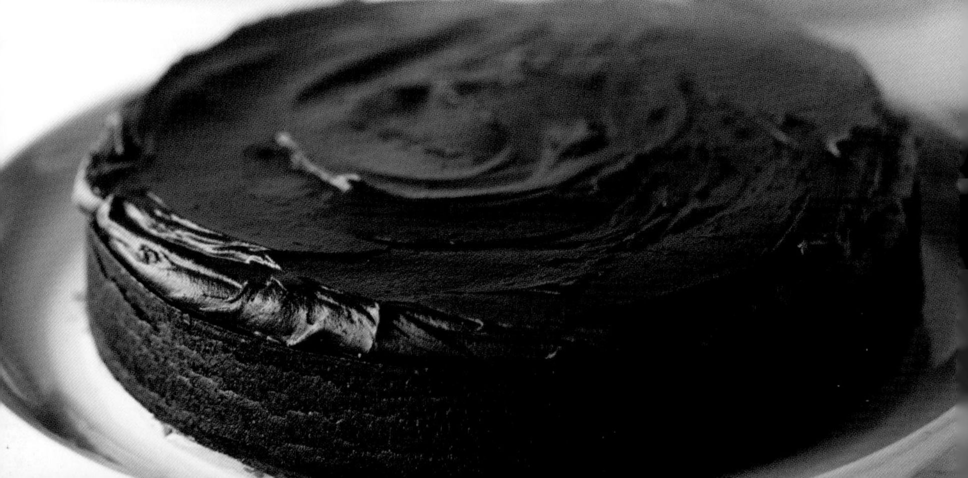

20 frosted carrot cake

Cake

- 1 cup (200 g) sugar
- 1 cup (200 g) brown sugar
- 3/4 cup (180 ml) vegetable oil
- 4 large eggs
- 2 teaspoons vanilla extract
- 2 cups (300 g) all-purpose (plain) flour
- 2 teaspoons cinnamon
- 2 tablespoons baking powder
- 1/2 teaspoon salt
- 1 pound (500 g) carrots, finely grated
- 1 cup (150 g) chopped pecans + extra, to decorate
- 1/4 cup (60 ml) dark rum

Frosting

- 1 pound (500 g) cream cheese, softened
- 1/2 cup (120 ml) honey
- 1 tablespoon finely grated untreated orange zest
- 2 cups (300 g) confectioners' (icing) sugar
- 1/2 cup (120 ml) heavy (double) cream

Cake Preheat the oven to 350°F (180°C/gas 4). Oil two deep 9-inch (23-cm) cake pans. Beat both sugars and the oil in a large bowl until creamy. Beat in the eggs and vanilla. Gradually stir in the flour, cinnamon, baking powder, and salt. Stir in the carrots, pecans, and rum. Divide between the pans. Bake for 35–40 minutes, until firm to the touch. Cool in the pans for 15 minutes. Peel off the paper. Let cool.

Frosting Beat the cream cheese, honey, orange zest, cream, and confectioners' sugar until smooth. Set a cake on a plate and spread with one-third of the frosting. Set the second cake on top and cover with one-third of the frosting. Spread the sides with frosting and top with the pecans. Chill for 2 hours before serving.

SERVES 8–12 • PREPARATION 30 MIN. + 2 HR. TO CHILL • COOKING 35–40 MIN. • LEVEL 2

1
christmas star cookies

2
valentine's day cookies

3
halloween cookies

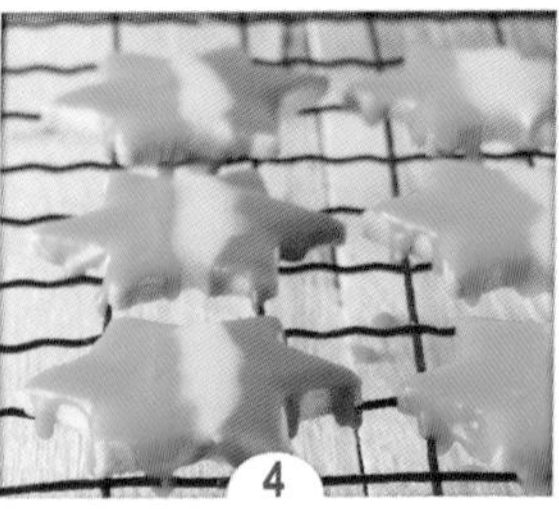
4
independence day cookies

5
chinese new year cookies

6
valentine's day cupcakes

7
easter bunny cupcakes

8
easter nest cupcakes

9
happy new year cupcakes

10
santa claus cupcakes

11
christmas cupcakes

12
yule log

13
rosh hashanah honey cake

14
passover fruit cake

holiday baking

15
simnel cake

16
tuscan grape harvest bread

17
bishops' cake

18
glazed christmas cake

19
galette des rois

20
florentine carnival cake

1 christmas star cookies

- $^{3}/_{4}$ cup (180 g) salted butter, softened
- $^{3}/_{4}$ cup (150 g) sugar
- 2 teaspoons vanilla extract (essence)
- 1 large egg + 1 large egg white
- 2 cups (300 g) all-purpose (plain) flour
- Sugar crystals or silver balls to decorate

Beat the butter and sugar with an electric mixer on medium speed until pale and creamy. Beat in the vanilla and 1 egg until just combined. With the mixer on low, gradually beat in the flour. Divide into two equal portions. Shape into disks, wrap in plastic wrap (cling film), and chill for 30 minutes.

Preheat the oven to 350°F (180°C/gas 4). Butter two baking sheets. Roll out the dough on a floured work surface to $^{1}/_{8}$ inch (3 mm) thick. Use a star-shaped cutter to cut out cookies. Transfer to the baking sheets. Bake for 10–12 minutes, until pale golden brown. Let cool on the baking sheets for 2–3 minutes. Transfer to racks and let cool completely. Brush with egg white and sprinkle with silver balls or sugar crystals.

MAKES 25–30 • PREPARATION 25 MIN. + 30 MIN. TO CHILL • COOKING 10–12 MIN. • LEVEL 1

2 valentine's day cookies

Cookies
- $^2/_3$ cup (100 g) all-purpose (plain) flour
- $^1/_4$ cup (30 g) cornstarch (cornflour)
- $^1/_4$ cup (60 g) salted butter
- $^1/_4$ cup (50 g) sugar
- 1 large egg, lightly beaten
- $^1/_2$ teaspoon vanilla extract (essence)
- Colored sugar sprinkles, to decorate

Vanilla Frosting
- 2 cups (300 g) confectioners' (icing) sugar
- 2 tablespoons salted butter, cut up
- $^1/_2$ teaspoon vanilla extract (essence)
- 2 tablespoons boiling water
- Few drops pink food coloring

Cookies Preheat oven to 350°F (180°C/gas 4). Line two baking sheets with parchment paper. Mix the flour and cornstarch in a bowl. Rub in the butter. Add the sugar, egg, and vanilla to make a stiff dough. Roll out the dough on a floured work surface to $^1/_8$ inch (3 mm) thick. Use a heart-shaped cookie cutter to cut out the cookies. Transfer to the baking sheets. Bake for 10–12 minutes, until golden brown. Let cool on wire racks.

Vanilla Frosting Put the confectioners' sugar, butter, and vanilla in a small bowl. Stir in the boiling water. Divide the frosting between two bowls. Color one bowl with the food coloring. Spread pink frosting on half the cookies. Top with the remaining cookies and spread with the plain frosting. Finish with sugar sprinkles.

MAKES 10–12 • PREPARATION 30 MIN. • COOKING 10–12 MIN. • LEVEL 2

3 halloween cookies

- $1\frac{1}{2}$ cups (225 g) all-purpose (plain) flour
- $\frac{1}{4}$ teaspoon baking soda (bicarbonate of soda)
- $\frac{1}{2}$ cup (120 g) salted butter, softened
- $\frac{1}{2}$ cup (100 g) firmly packed light brown sugar
- 1 large egg
- 2 ounces (60 g) dark chocolate, coarsely chopped
- 8 ounces (250 g) store-bought ready-to-roll white fondant
- 2 drops orange food coloring (or red and yellow)
- Edible black candy writer, to decorate

Mix the flour and baking soda in a medium bowl. Beat the butter and brown sugar in a large bowl with an electric mixer on medium speed until creamy. Add the egg, beating until just blended.

Melt the chocolate in a double boiler over barely simmering water. Stir the chocolate into the butter mixture. Mix in the dry ingredients. Press the dough into a disk, wrap in plastic wrap (cling film), and refrigerate for 30 minutes.

Preheat the oven to 350°F (180°C/gas 4). Butter two baking sheets. Roll out the dough on a lightly floured surface to $\frac{1}{4}$-inch (5 mm) thick. Use a 3-inch (8-cm) cookie cutter to cut out the cookies. Transfer to the baking sheets, spacing well. Bake until firm, 10–15 minutes. Transfer to racks and let cool completely.

Knead the fondant until soft. Divide it in half. Place one portion in a bowl and mix in the orange food coloring. Roll out the plain fondant on a surface dusted with confectioners' sugar to $\frac{1}{8}$-inch (3-mm) thick. Use the cookie cutter to cut out enough fondant rounds to cover half the cookies. Brush the fondant rounds with water. Place wet-side down on half the cookies. Repeat with the orange fondant and place on the remaining cookies. Use an edible black candy writer to draw Jack-o-lanterns and spooky designs on the cookies.

MAKES 12–16 • PREPARATION 30 MIN. + 30 MIN. TO CHILL • COOKING 10–15 MIN. • LEVEL 2

4 independence day cookies

- 1 cup (150 g) all-purpose (plain) flour
- 2/3 cup (100 g) rice flour
- 3/4 cup (150 g) superfine (caster) sugar
- 1/2 cup (120 g) salted butter
- 1 large egg yolk
- 2 tablespoons heavy (double) cream
- 1 recipe vanilla frosting (see page 121)
- Few drops red food coloring
- Few drops blue food coloring

Preheat the oven to 375°F (190°C/gas 5). Line two baking sheets with parchment paper. Mix both flours with the sugar in a medium bowl. Rub in the butter. Beat the egg yolk and bind the mixture with this and the cream to make a very stiff paste. Roll out to 1/4 inch (5 mm) thick and use a star-shaped cutter to cut out cookies. Transfer to the prepared baking sheets, spacing well. Bake until pale golden brown, 10–15 minutes. Transfer to wire racks and let cool completely.

Prepare the vanilla frosting. Divide evenly among three small bowls. Color one bowl with red food coloring, one bowl with blue food coloring, and leave one plain. Decorate the cookies with the colored glazes so that they recall the American flag.

MAKES 30–32 • PREPARATION 30 MIN. • COOKING 10–15 MIN. • LEVEL 1

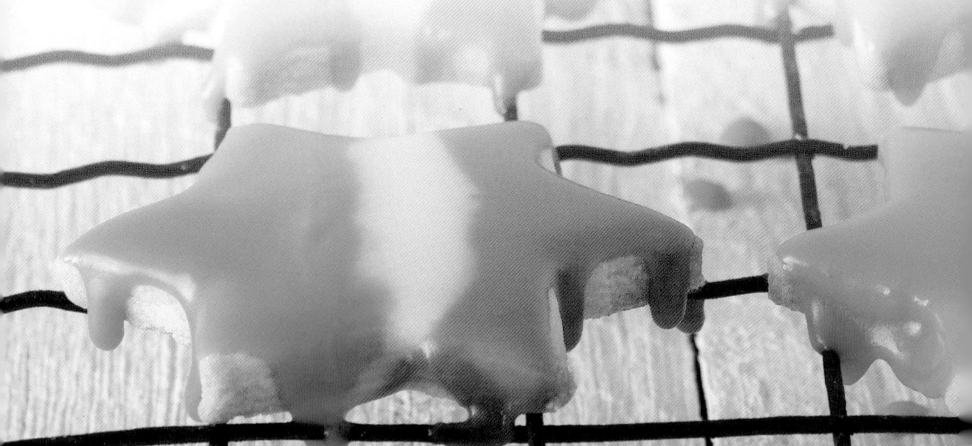

5 chinese new year cookies

- $2\frac{1}{2}$ cups (450 g) all-purpose (plain) flour
- $\frac{1}{2}$ teaspoon baking powder
- $\frac{1}{2}$ teaspoon baking soda (bicarbonate of soda)
- $\frac{3}{4}$ cup (180 g) salted butter, softened
- $\frac{3}{4}$ cup (150 g) superfine (caster) sugar
- 1 large egg
- 1 teaspoon almond extract (essence)
- 30 whole blanched almonds to decorate

Preheat the oven to 350°F (180°C/gas 4). Line two baking sheets with parchment paper. Combine the flour, baking powder, and baking soda in a medium bowl. Beat the butter and sugar in a medium bowl with an electric mixer on medium speed until pale and creamy. Add the egg and almond extract and beat until incorporated. With the mixer on low speed, gradually add the flour mixture, beating until just combined. Shape the dough into 30 balls. Arrange on the prepared baking sheets, spacing them 1 inch (2.5 cm) apart. Press your thumb in the center of each cookie to make an indent and place an almond in the hollow.

Bake for 10–15 minutes, until golden brown. Cool on the sheets until the cookies firm slightly, 2–3 minutes. Transfer to racks and let cool completely.

MAKES 30 • PREPARATION 15 MIN. • COOKING 10–15 MIN. • LEVEL 1

6 valentine's day cupcakes

Cupcakes
- $1\frac{1}{4}$ cups (180 g) all-purpose (plain) flour
- 3 tablespoons unsweetened cocoa powder, sifted
- $1\frac{1}{2}$ teaspoons baking powder
- 1 teaspoon ground cinnamon
- $\frac{1}{8}$ teaspoon salt
- $\frac{1}{2}$ cup (120 g) unsalted butter, softened
- $\frac{3}{4}$ cup (150 g) sugar
- $\frac{1}{2}$ teaspoon vanilla extract (essence)
- 2 large eggs
- $\frac{1}{3}$ cup (90 ml) milk
- $\frac{1}{2}$ cup (120 g) fresh or frozen (thawed) strawberries
- $\frac{1}{2}$ cup (90 g) dark chocolate chips

White Chocolate Buttercream
- 3 ounces (90 g) white chocolate
- $\frac{1}{2}$ cup (120 g) unsalted butter, softened
- $\frac{1}{4}$ teaspoon vanilla extract (essence)
- $\frac{1}{2}$ tablespoon milk
- 1 cup (150 g) confectioners' (icing) sugar
- Few drops pink food coloring
- Confectionery hearts, to decorate

Cupcakes Preheat the oven to 350°F (180°C/gas 4). Line a standard 12-cup muffin tin with paper liners. Combine the flour, cocoa, baking powder, cinnamon, and salt in a small bowl. Beat the butter, sugar, and vanilla in a medium bowl with an electric mixer on medium speed until pale and creamy. Add the eggs one at a time, beating until just blended after each addition. With the mixer on low speed, add the mixed dry ingredients, alternating with the milk. Stir the strawberries and chocolate chips in by hand.

Spoon the batter into the prepared cups. Bake for 20–25 minutes, until risen and firm to the touch. Transfer to a wire rack. Let cool completely.

White Chocolate Buttercream Melt the chocolate in a double boiler over barely simmering water. Remove from the heat and let cool. Beat the butter and vanilla in a medium bowl with an electric mixer on medium speed until pale and creamy. Add the milk and cooled chocolate, beating until blended. Gradually add the confectioners' sugar, beating until blended. Tint pink with a few drops of food coloring. Spoon the buttercream into a pastry bag fitted with a star-shaped nozzle. Pipe a rosette on top of each cupcake and sprinkle with confectionery hearts.

MAKES 12 • PREPARATION 30 MIN. • COOKING 20–25 MIN. • LEVEL 1

7 easter bunny cupcakes

Cupcakes
- 3 ounces (90 g) dark chocolate
- 1/4 cup (60 g) salted butter
- 1/2 teaspoon peppermint extract (essence)
- 1 1/2 cups (225 g) all-purpose (plain) flour
- 3/4 cup (150 g) firmly packed light brown sugar
- 2 tablespoons unsweetened cocoa powder
- 1 1/2 teaspoons baking powder
- 1 teaspoon baking soda (bicarbonate of soda)
- 1 cup (250 ml) milk

White Mint Ganache
- 4 ounces (120 g) white chocolate, coarsely chopped
- 1/4 cup (60 ml) light (single) cream
- 1/4 teaspoon peppermint extract (essence)

To Decorate
- 2 ounces (60 g) milk chocolate, melted, to decorate
- 12 silver balls

Cupcakes Preheat the oven to 325°F (170°C/gas 3). Line a 12-cup muffin tin with paper liners. Melt the chocolate, butter, and peppermint in a double boiler over barely simmering water. Combine the flour, brown sugar, cocoa, baking powder, and baking soda in a bowl. Stir in the chocolate mixture and milk. Spoon into the cups. Bake for 25–30 minutes, until firm. Transfer to a rack.

White Mint Ganache Melt the chocolate and cream in a double boiler over barely simmering water. Stir in the peppermint and let cool. Spread over the cupcakes.

To Decorate Spoon the melted milk chocolate into an envelope and snip off a corner using scissors. Pipe rabbits on the cupcakes. Place a silver ball for the tail.

MAKES 12 • PREPARATION 30 MIN. • COOKING 25–30 MIN. • LEVEL 2

8 easter nest cupcakes

Cupcakes
- 1 recipe Easter bunny cupcakes (see recipe on facing page)

Chocolate Buttercream
- 3 ounces (90 g) dark chocolate
- ½ cup (120 g) unsalted butter, softened
- ¼ teaspoon vanilla extract (essence)
- ½ tablespoon milk
- 1 cup (150 g) confectioners' (icing) sugar

To Decorate
- 3 small flaky chocolate bars, to decorate, crumbled
- 12 mini speckled Easter eggs, to decorate

Cupcakes Prepare the cupcakes and set aside to cool.

Chocolate Buttercream Melt the chocolate in a double boiler over barely simmering water. Set aside to cool. Beat the butter and vanilla in a small bowl with an electric mixer on medium speed until pale and creamy. Pour in the milk and chocolate, beating until blended. Gradually add the confectioners' sugar, beating until blended. Spread the buttercream on the cupcakes.

To Decorate Break the flaked chocolate bars into small pieces and use to create nests on top of the cupcakes. Place eggs in each nest.

MAKES 12 • PREPARATION 30 MIN. • COOKING 25–30 MIN. • LEVEL 2

9 happy new year cupcakes

Cupcakes
- $1\frac{1}{3}$ cups (200 g) all-purpose (plain) flour
- $\frac{1}{3}$ cup (50 g) ground almonds
- $1\frac{1}{2}$ teaspoons baking powder
- $\frac{1}{2}$ teaspoon ground cinnamon
- $\frac{1}{8}$ teaspoon salt
- 1 cup (200 g) sugar
- 2 large eggs
- 1 teaspoon finely grated orange zest
- 1 teaspoon vanilla extract (essence)
- 1 cup (250 ml) light (single) cream
- 12 milk chocolate squares
- Small cachous, to decorate
- 12 sparklers, to decorate

Chocolate Ganache
- 8 ounces (250 g) dark chocolate, coarsely chopped
- $\frac{1}{2}$ cup (60 ml) heavy (double) cream

Cupcakes Preheat the oven to 350°F (180°C/gas 4). Line a standard 12-cup muffin tin with silver paper liners or foil cups. Combine the flour, almonds, baking powder, cinnamon, and salt in a small bowl. Beat the sugar, eggs, orange zest, and vanilla in a medium bowl with an electric mixer on medium speed until pale and creamy. With the mixer on low speed, gradually add the flour mixture and cream.

Spoon half the batter into the prepared cups. Place a chocolate square in the center of each one and spoon in the remaining batter. Bake for 20–25 minutes, until golden brown and firm to the touch. Transfer the muffin tin to a wire rack. Let cool completely before removing the cupcakes.

Chocolate Ganache Melt the chocolate and cream in a double boiler over barely simmering water, stirring until smooth. Remove from the heat and let cool. Spread the ganache over the cupcakes and sprinkle with cachous. Cut the sparklers down to a shorter size and insert into the cupcakes. Light when ready to serve.

MAKES 12 • PREPARATION 30 MIN. • COOKING 20–25 MIN. • LEVEL 2

Children will especially enjoy these cupcakes. Be sure to remove the sparklers before they burn down to the ganache.

10 santa claus cupcakes

- 3 ounces (90 g) dark chocolate, coarsely chopped
- 1/3 cup (90 ml) light (single) cream
- 2/3 cup (100 g) all-purpose (plain) flour
- 1/2 cup (50 g) ground almonds
- 2 tablespoons unsweetened cocoa powder
- 1 teaspoon baking powder
- 1/3 cup (90 g) salted butter, softened
- 1 cup (200 g) sugar
- 2 large eggs
- 1 recipe white chocolate buttercream (see page 126)
- 12 chocolate Santa Claus

Preheat the oven to 350°F (180°C/gas 4). Line a 12-cup muffin tin with paper liners. Melt the chocolate and cream in a double boiler over barely simmering water.

Combine the flour, almonds, cocoa, and baking powder in a bowl. Beat the butter and sugar with an electric mixer on medium speed until pale and creamy. Add the eggs one at a time, beating until just blended. Beat in the flour mixture and chocolate. Spoon into the cups.

Bake for 20–25 minutes, until golden brown and firm to the touch. Transfer the muffin tin to a wire rack. Let cool. Spread the buttercream over the cupcakes. Press a chocolate Santa into each cupcake.

MAKES 12 • PREPARATION 30 MIN. • COOKING 20–25 MIN. • LEVEL 2

11 christmas cupcakes

- 2 cups (200 g) chopped mixed candied fruit
- 1½ cups (375 ml) white grape juice
- ¾ cup (150 g) firmly packed dark brown sugar
- 2½ cups (375 g) all-purpose (plain) flour
- 1½ teaspoons baking powder
- 1 teaspoon baking soda (bicarbonate of soda)
- 1 teaspoon ground cinnamon
- 1 teaspoon ground nutmeg
- ½ teaspoon salt
- 2 large egg whites, lightly beaten
- ¼ cup (60 ml) vegetable oil
- ⅓ cup (90 ml) milk
- 4 tablespoons (60 ml) brandy
- 1 pound (500 g) marzipan, softened
- Holly-shaped candy

Stir the candied fruit, grape juice, and brown sugar in a large bowl. Cover and set aside for 8 hours.

Preheat the oven to 300°F (150°C/gas 2). Line two standard 12-cup muffin tins with paper liners. Mix the flour, baking powder, baking soda, cinnamon, nutmeg, and salt in a large bowl. Stir the egg whites, oil, milk, and 2 tablespoons brandy into the fruit mixture. Stir in the dry ingredients. Spoon into the cups. Bake for 75–80 minutes, until a toothpick inserted into the center comes out clean. Drizzle the hot cupcakes with the remaining brandy. Cool completely in the pan.

Dust a work surface with confectioners' sugar. Roll out the marzipan and cut out 18–20 disks to cover the cupcakes. Decorate with the holly-shaped candy.

MAKES 18–20 • PREPARATION 30 MIN. + 8 HR. TO STEEP • COOKING 75–80 MIN. • LEVEL 2

12 yule log

Cake
- 1/2 cup (75 g) all-purpose (plain) flour
- 2 tablespoons unsweetened cocoa powder
- 1 teaspoon ground cinnamon
- 4 large eggs
- 1/2 cup (100 g) superfine (caster) sugar + extra, to sprinkle
- 1 teaspoon vanilla extract (essence)
- 2 tablespoons butter, melted and cooled

Filling
- 1/2 cup (120 ml) heavy (double) cream
- 1 (8-ounce/250-g) can sweetened chestnut purée
- 1/4 cup (40 g) hazelnuts, toasted and finely chopped

Chocolate Buttercream
- 4 ounces (120 g) dark chocolate
- 1 cup (250 g) salted butter, softened
- 1/2 teaspoon vanilla extract (essence)
- 3 cups (450 g) confectioners' (icing) sugar

Cake Preheat the oven to 350°F (180°C/gas 4). Line a jelly-roll pan with parchment paper. Sift the flour, cocoa, and cinnamon into a bowl. Beat the eggs, sugar, and vanilla with an electric mixer on medium speed until thick, creamy, and tripled in volume. Fold in the flour mixture. Fold in the melted butter. Spoon the batter into the prepared pan. Bake for 15–20 minutes, until the sponge springs back when gently pressed. Lay a clean kitchen towel on a work surface and sprinkle with sugar. Turn the cake out onto the towel. Roll up lengthwise and place on a wire rack, seam-side down.

Filling Beat the cream in a small bowl until soft peaks form. Stir in the chestnut purée. Unroll the cake, peel away the paper, and spread with the filling. Sprinkle with the hazelnuts, re-roll, and trim the ends. Place the cake on a large serving plate. Diagonally cut 4 inches (10 cm) off one end and place it along the log to resemble a branch. Place in the refrigerator.

Chocolate Buttercream Melt the chocolate in a double boiler over barely simmering water. Let cool. Beat the butter and vanilla with an electric mixer on medium speed until pale and creamy. Stir in the chocolate. Gradually beat in the confectioners' sugar.

Spread the buttercream over the Yule log. Using the prongs of a fork, create a bark pattern.

SERVES 8–10 • PREPARATION 1 HR. • COOKING 15–20 MIN. • LEVEL 2

13 rosh hashanah honey cake

- 3 cups (450 g) all purpose (plain) flour
- 3 teaspoons baking powder
- $1\frac{1}{2}$ teaspoons ground ginger
- 1 teaspoon ground cinnamon
- 1 teaspoon baking soda (bicarbonate of soda)
- $\frac{1}{2}$ teaspoon ground cloves
- 1 cup (250 ml) honey
- 1 cup (250 ml) water
- 1 cup (250 ml) rice bran oil
- 1 cup (200 g) firmly packed brown sugar
- 2 large eggs, lightly beaten
- 1 teaspoon vanilla extract (essence)
- Confectioners' (icing) sugar, to dust

Preheat the oven to 325°F (170°C/gas 3). Grease a 5 x 9-inch (12 x 24-cm) loaf pan and line with parchment paper. Mix the flour, baking powder, ginger, cinnamon, baking soda, and cloves in a bowl. Combine the honey, water, and oil in a small saucepan over low heat and bring to a boil. Remove from the heat and set aside.

Beat the sugar, eggs, and vanilla in a medium bowl with an electric mixer on medium speed until thick. With the mixer on low speed, add the flour and honey mixtures. Spoon the batter into the prepared pan.

Bake for $1\frac{1}{4}$ hours, until a toothpick inserted into the center comes our clean. Let cool in the pan for 10 minutes, then turn out onto a wire rack and let cool completely. Dust with confectioners' sugar.

SERVES 10–12 • PREPARATION 30 MIN. • COOKING $1\frac{1}{4}$ HR. • LEVEL 1

14 passover fruit cake

- $\frac{3}{4}$ cup (130 g) raisins
- $\frac{3}{4}$ cup (130 g) currants
- $\frac{3}{4}$ cup (130 g) golden raisins (sultanas)
- $\frac{1}{4}$ cup (45 g) candied (glacé) red and green cherries, coarsely chopped
- $\frac{1}{4}$ cup (25 g) chopped mixed peel
- $\frac{1}{3}$ cup (90 ml) sweet sherry
- 1 cup (250 g) salted butter, softened
- 1 cup (200 g) firmly packed brown sugar
- 4 large eggs
- $1\frac{1}{2}$ cups (225 g) ground almonds
- 1 teaspoon ground cinnamon
- $\frac{1}{2}$ teaspoon ground nutmeg
- $\frac{1}{2}$ teaspoon ground ginger
- $\frac{1}{3}$ cup (50 g) slivered almonds

Combine the raisins, currants, golden raisins, cherries, mixed peel, and sherry in a bowl. Let steep overnight.

Preheat the oven to 350°F (180°C/gas 4). Grease a deep 8-inch (20-cm) round pan. Line with parchment paper. Beat the butter and sugar with an electric mixer on medium speed until creamy. Add the eggs one at a time, beating until just blended after each addition.

Combine the ground almonds, cinnamon, nutmeg, and ginger in a bowl. Stir into the batter followed by the soaked fruits. Spoon into the prepared pan and sprinkle with the slivered almonds. Bake for $1\frac{1}{2}$ hours, until a toothpick inserted into the center comes our clean. Let cool in the pan on a wire rack.

SERVES 8–12 • PREPARATION 20–25 MIN. + 12 HR. TO STEEP • COOKING $1\frac{1}{2}$ HR. • LEVEL 1

15 simnel cake

- 3/4 cup (135 g) raisins
- 3/4 cup (135 g) currants
- 1/2 cup (90 g) pitted prunes, coarsely chopped
- 1/2 cup (90 g) red and green candied (glacé) cherries, coarsely chopped
- 1/2 cup (50 g) chopped mixed peel
- 1/3 cup (90 ml) sweet sherry, brandy, or whisky
- 1 1/2 pounds (750 g) marzipan
- 2 cups (300 g) all-purpose (plain) flour
- 2 teaspoons baking powder
- 1 teaspoon ground cinnamon
- 1/2 teaspoon ground nutmeg
- 1 cup (200 g) firmly packed light brown sugar
- 3/4 cup (180 g) salted butter, softened
- 1 teaspoon finely grated organic orange zest
- 3 large eggs
- 2 tablespoons apricot preserves (jam), warmed

Put the raisins, currants, prunes, cherries, mixed peel and sherry in a bowl. Set aside overnight to steep.

Shape the marzipan into three different-size balls, weighing 12 ounces (350 g), 8 ounces (250 g), and 5 ounces (150 g). Wrap in plastic wrap (cling film) and refrigerate for 1 hour until firm. Dust a work surface with confectioners' sugar. Roll the medium-size ball of marzipan out and cut into an 8-inch (20-cm) disk.

Preheat the oven to 300°F (150°C/gas 2). Grease a deep 8-inch (20-cm) round cake pan. Line the base and sides with a triple layer of parchment paper. Mix the flour, baking powder, cinnamon, and nutmeg in a bowl. Beat the sugar, butter, and orange zest in a bowl with an electric mixer on medium speed until creamy. Add the eggs one at a time, beating until just blended after each addition. With the mixer on low speed, beat in the flour mixture and soaked fruits. Pour half the batter into the prepared pan. Place the disk of marzipan on top. Spoon in the remaining batter. Bake for 2 hours, until a toothpick inserted into the center comes out clean. Let cool in the pan for 20 minutes. Turn out onto a wire rack and let cool. Brush with the preserves.

Roll the larger ball of marzipan out and cut a 10-inch (25-cm) disk. Place on the cake. Shape twelve small balls from the remaining marzipan and arrange on top.

SERVES 12–14 • PREPARATION 45 MIN. + 12 HR. TO STEEP • COOKING 2 HR. • LEVEL 2

16 tuscan grape harvest bread

- 1 ounce (30 g) compressed fresh yeast or 2 ($\frac{1}{4}$-ounce/ 7-g) packages active dry yeast
- $1\frac{1}{4}$ cups (300 ml) lukewarm water + extra, as required
- 3 cups (450 g) all-purpose (plain) flour
- $\frac{1}{4}$ cup (50 g) sugar
- $\frac{1}{4}$ teaspoon salt
- 1 pound (500 g) black grapes (preferably seedless), lightly crushed
- $\frac{3}{4}$ cup (150 g) sugar
- Confectioners' (icing) sugar, to dust

Butter a large baking sheet. Line with parchment paper. Stir the yeast and water in a small bowl. Set aside until frothy, 5–10 minutes. Combine the flour, sugar, and salt in a large bowl. Stir in the yeast mixture. Knead until smooth and elastic, about 10 minutes. Shape into a ball. Set aside until doubled in bulk, about 1 hour.

Divide the dough in two. Roll out to 1 inch (2.5 cm) thick. Place one piece on the baking sheet. Cover with half the grapes and sprinkle with half the sugar. Top with the remaining dough. Spread with the remaining grapes. Sprinkle with the remaining sugar. Let rise for 1 hour. Preheat the oven to 350°F (180°C/gas 4). Bake for 40–50 minutes, until golden. Serve warm, dusted with confectioners' sugar.

SERVES 8–10 • PREPARATION 30 MIN. + 2 HR. TO RISE • COOKING 40–50 MIN. • LEVEL 2

17 bishops' cake

- ½ cup (120 g) mixed candied (glacé) fruit, such as pineapple, pears, and apricots, coarsely chopped
- ¾ cup (120 g) cashew nuts
- ¾ cup (120 g) Brazil nuts
- ¾ cup (90 g) walnut halves
- ½ cup (90 g) raisins
- ⅓ cup (60 g) red and green candied (glacé) cherries
- ¼ cup (45 g) dried pitted dates
- 2 tablespoons mixed peel
- ½ cup (75 g) all-purpose (plain) flour
- ½ teaspoon baking powder
- ½ cup (100 g) sugar
- 2 large eggs, lightly beaten
- ¼ cup (60 ml) brandy
- 1 teaspoon vanilla extract (essence)

Preheat the oven to 275°F (140°C/gas 1). Grease a 9 x 4-inch (23 x 10-cm) loaf pan and line with parchment paper. Combine three-quarters of the fruit and nuts in a large bowl. Add the flour and baking powder and stir to coat. Beat the sugar, eggs, brandy, and vanilla with an electric mixer on low speed until combined. Add to the fruit mixture and mix well. Spoon the batter into the prepared pan. Top with the remaining fruit and nuts.

Bake for 2½ hours, until a toothpick inserted into the center comes out clean. Cover the top with aluminum foil if it begins to brown too much. Leave to cool in the pan for 10 minutes, then turn out onto a wire rack and let cool completely.

SERVES 8–10 • PREPARATION 30 MIN. • COOKING 2½ HR. • LEVEL 2

18 glazed christmas cake

Cake

- 1 cup (180 g) raisins
- 1 cup (180 g) currants
- 1 cup (180 g) golden raisins (sultanas)
- 2/3 cup (120 g) candied (glacé) green and red cherries
- 1/3 cup (60 g) dried apricots, coarsely chopped
- 1/3 cup (30 g) mixed peel
- 1/2 cup (120 ml) brandy
- 3/4 cup (180 g) salted butter
- 1 cup (200 g) firmly packed dark brown sugar
- 4 large eggs
- 1 1/2 cups (225 g) all-purpose (plain) flour
- 1 teaspoon pumpkin pie spice (allspice)
- 1 teaspoon ground cinnamon
- 1/2 teaspoon ground ginger
- 1/3 cup (50 g) blanched almonds, coarsely chopped
- 1/3 cup (50 g) Brazil nuts, coarsely chopped

Fruit Glaze

- 1/2 cup (90 g) candied (glacé) green and red cherries
- 1/2 cup (90 g) candied (glacé) pineapple, coarsely chopped
- 1/4 cup (40 g) blanched almonds
- 1/4 cup (40 g) Brazil nuts
- 1/4 cup (30 g) walnut halves
- 1/2 cup (150 g) apricot preserves (jam), warmed

Cake Combine the raisins, currants, golden raisins, cherries, apricots, mixed peel, and 1/3 cup (90 ml) of the brandy in a medium bowl. Let steep overnight.

Preheat the oven to 300°F (150°C/gas 2). Grease a deep 8-inch (20-cm) round cake pan. Line the base and sides with a triple layer of parchment paper, extending 5 inches (13 cm) above the rim.

Beat the butter and sugar in a large bowl with an electric mixer on medium speed until creamy. Add the eggs one at a time, beating until just blended after each addition. Combine the flour, pumpkin pie spice, cinnamon, and ginger in a small bowl. Add the flour mixture, soaked fruits, and nuts alternately, stirring to combine. Spoon the batter into the prepared pan.

Bake for 3 1/2 hours, until a skewer comes out clean when inserted into the center. Remove the cake from the oven and prick the top several times with a skewer. Drizzle with the remaining brandy and leave to cool in the pan.

Fruit Glaze Combine the cherries, pineapple, almonds, Brazil nuts, and walnuts in a medium bowl. Brush the top of the cake with apricot preserves and decorate with the candied fruit and nut mixture. Glaze with the remaining preserves.

SERVES 10–12 • PREPARATION 30 MIN. + 12 HR. TO STEEP • COOKING 3 1/2 HR. • LEVEL 2

19 galette des rois

- 2 (8-ounce/250-g) sheets ready-rolled puff pastry
- ½ cup (120 g) butter, softened
- ⅓ cup (70 g) superfine (caster) sugar
- ½ cup (75 g) ground almonds
- 3 large egg yolks, lightly beaten + 1 large egg, lightly beaten, to glaze
- 1 tablespoon kirsch
- ½ teaspoon almond extract (essence)
- 1 dried bean

Preheat the oven to 400°F (200°C/ gas 6). Lightly grease a baking sheet. Cut out a 10-inch (25-cm) circle from one sheet of pastry and place on the baking sheet. Beat the butter and sugar until pale and creamy. Add the almonds, egg yolks, kirsch, almond extract, and bean. Spread on the pastry. Brush the edge with egg.

Cut out an 11-inch (28-cm) circle from the remaining sheet of pastry and place on top of the other round. Press to seal and trim to size. Glaze the top with the remaining egg. Bake for 30–35 minutes, until golden brown. Serve warm or at room temperature.

SERVES 8–10 • PREPARATION 30 MIN. • COOKING 30–35 MIN. • LEVEL 2

20 florentine carnival cake

- 1 ounce (30 g) compressed fresh yeast or 2 (¼-ounce/7-g) packages active dry yeast
- 1 cup (250 ml) lukewarm water
- 3 cups (450 g) all-purpose (plain) flour
- 1 cup (200 g) sugar
- 4 large egg yolks
- ⅓ cup (90 g) unsalted butter, melted
- 2 tablespoons finely grated untreated orange zest
- ¼ teaspoon salt
- Confectioners' sugar, to dust

Butter a jelly-roll pan. Line with parchment paper. Mix the yeast in ½ cup (120 ml) of water. Set aside until frothy, 5–10 minutes. Mix the flour and sugar in a bowl. Add the yeast mixture and remaining water and stir until smooth. Transfer to a work surface and knead until smooth and elastic, about 10 minutes. Shape into a ball. Cover and let rise in a warm place for about 1 hour.

Knead the dough again, gradually working in the egg yolks, butter, orange zest, and salt. Place in the pan. Let rise until doubled in bulk, about 2 hours. Preheat the oven to 350°F (180°C/gas 4). Bake for 25–35 minutes, until golden. Cool in the pan for 15 minutes. Dust with confectioners' sugar just before serving.

SERVES 10–12 • PREPARATION 30 MIN. + 3 HR. TO RISE • COOKING 25–35 MIN. • LEVEL 2

1

white chocolate chip cookies

2

chocolate pecan cookies

3

chocolate peanut cookies

4

cinnamon fudge brownies

5

cappuccino brownies

6

mocha & pecan brownies

7

chocolate coconut cupcakes

8

marbled chocolate cupcakes

9

chocolate mint cupcakes

10

chocolate meringues

11

florentines

12
chocolate macaroons

13
chocolate caramel tart

14
bittersweet chocolate tart

chocolate

15
chocolate cranberry tart

16
chocolate layer cake

17
chocolate beet cake

18
chocolate mayonnaise cake

19
marbled cheesecake

20
chocolate whiskey cake

1 white chocolate chip cookies

- $1\frac{2}{3}$ cups (250 g) all-purpose (plain) flour
- $1\frac{1}{2}$ teaspoons baking powder
- $\frac{1}{2}$ cup (125 g) salted butter, softened
- $\frac{1}{4}$ cup (60 ml) sunflower or peanut oil
- $\frac{3}{4}$ cup (150 g) firmly packed light brown sugar
- 1 large egg
- $\frac{1}{2}$ teaspoon vanilla extract (essence)
- 1 cup (180 g) white chocolate chips
- 1 cup (120 g) chopped walnuts

Mix the flour and baking powder in a medium bowl. Beat the butter, oil, and brown sugar in a large bowl with an electric mixer on medium speed until creamy. Add the egg and vanilla, beating until just blended. Beat in the flour mixture, chocolate chips, and walnuts. Form the dough into a 7-inch (18-cm) long log, wrap in plastic wrap (cling film), and chill for 30 minutes.

Preheat the oven to 375°F (190°C/gas 5). Butter two baking sheets. Slice the dough $\frac{1}{4}$ inch (5-mm) thick and place 2 inches (5 cm) apart on the prepared baking sheets. Bake for 8–10 minutes, until just golden at the edges. Transfer to racks to cool.

MAKES 25–30 • PREPARATION 20 MIN. + 30 MIN. TO CHILL • COOKING 8–10 MIN. • LEVEL 1

2 chocolate pecan cookies

Cookies
- $1\frac{1}{3}$ cups (200 g) all-purpose (plain) flour
- $\frac{1}{2}$ teaspoon baking soda (bicarbonate of soda)
- 2 ounces (60 g) dark chocolate, coarsely chopped
- $\frac{1}{2}$ cup (125 g) salted butter, softened
- 1 cup (200 g) sugar
- 1 teaspoon vanilla extract (essence)
- 1 large egg
- 2 tablespoons milk

Chocolate Frosting
- 4 ounces (120 g) dark chocolate, coarsely chopped
- $\frac{1}{4}$ cup (60 g) salted butter, softened
- $1\frac{1}{3}$ cups (200 g) confectioners' (icing) sugar
- About 16 pecans, halved

Cookies Preheat the oven to 400°F (200°C/gas 6). Butter three baking sheets. Mix the flour and baking soda in a bowl. Melt the chocolate in a double boiler over barely simmering water. Beat the butter, sugar, and chocolate in a bowl with an electric mixer on medium speed until creamy. Add the vanilla and egg, beating until just blended. With the mixer on low speed, beat in the flour mixture and milk.

Drop teaspoons of the dough 1 inch (2.5 cm) apart on the prepared baking sheets. Bake for 10–12 minutes, until slightly risen. Cool on the sheets until slightly firm, 2–3 minutes. Transfer to wire racks to cool completely.

Frosting Melt the chocolate in a double boiler over barely simmering water. Add the butter and stir until smooth. Beat in the confectioners' sugar. Spread the cookies with frosting and top with half a pecan.

MAKES 30–32 • PREPARATION 20 MIN. • COOKING 10–12 MIN. • LEVEL 1

3 chocolate peanut cookies

- 1 cup (250 g) chunky peanut butter
- 1/4 cup (60 ml) canola oil
- 1/2 cup (100 g) firmly packed dark brown sugar
- 1/2 cup (100 g) sugar
- 2 large eggs
- 3 tablespoons plain yogurt
- 2 teaspoons vanilla extract (essence)
- 3/4 cup (120 g) all-purpose (plain) flour
- 1/3 cup (50 g) unsweetened cocoa powder
- 1/4 cup (40 g) rolled oats
- 1 teaspoon baking soda (bicarbonate of soda)
- 1/2 teaspoon salt
- 1/2 cup (90 g) dark chocolate chips
- 1/4 cup (50 g) raw sugar

Preheat the oven to 350°F (180°C/gas 4). Set out two large baking sheets.

Beat the peanut butter, oil, and both sugars in a large bowl with an electric mixer on medium speed until creamy. Beat in the eggs, yogurt, and vanilla until just combined.

Mix the flour, cocoa, oats, baking soda, and salt in a medium bowl. With the mixer on low speed, gradually beat the flour mixture into the peanut butter mixture until blended. Stir in the chocolate chips.

Drop slightly rounded tablespoons of the dough onto the prepared baking sheets, spacing about 2 inches (5 cm) apart. Sprinkle with the raw sugar.

Bake the cookies for 10–15 minutes, until set and the tops look cracked. Cool on the sheets until slightly firm, 2–3 minutes. Transfer to wire racks to cool completely.

MAKES 25–30 • PREPARATION 15 MIN. • COOKING 10–15 MIN.
LEVEL 1

These cookies are slightly chewy and perfect with a morning cup of tea or coffee. Adjust the baking time to get the right level of chewiness.

4 cinnamon fudge brownies

Brownies
- $\frac{1}{2}$ cup (75 g) all-purpose (plain) flour
- $1\frac{1}{2}$ teaspoons ground cinnamon
- 6 ounces (180 g) dark chocolate, chopped
- $\frac{3}{4}$ cup (180 g) salted butter
- 4 large eggs
- 1 cup (200 g) sugar
- $1\frac{1}{2}$ teaspoons vanilla extract (essence)
- 1 cup (120 g) coarsely chopped walnuts

Dark Chocolate Ganache
- 6 ounces (180 g) dark chocolate, chopped
- 3 tablespoons unsalted butter
- 2 tablespoons heavy (double) cream

Brownies Preheat the oven to 350°F (180°C/gas 4). Butter an 8-inch (20-cm) square baking pan. Mix the flour and cinnamon in a small bowl. Melt the chocolate and butter in a double boiler over barely simmering water. Turn off the heat and let stand over the water.

Beat the eggs and sugar in large bowl until thick and creamy. Beat in the vanilla. Fold in the flour mixture. Gradually add the chocolate to the egg mixture, beating until just combined. Stir in the walnuts. Pour into the prepared pan. Bake for 30–35 minutes, until the top is set and a toothpick inserted into center comes out with a few moist crumbs attached. Cool in the pan on a rack.

Dark Chocolate Ganache Whisk the chocolate, butter, and cream in a small saucepan over low heat until smooth. Pour evenly over the brownies in the pan.

MAKES 12–16 • PREPARATION 20 MIN. • COOKING 30–35 MIN. • LEVEL 1

5 cappuccino brownies

- $\frac{1}{2}$ cup (120 g) salted butter, diced
- 3 ounces (90 g) dark chocolate, chopped
- $1\frac{1}{2}$ cups (300 g) sugar
- 3 large eggs
- $\frac{3}{4}$ cup (120 g) all-purpose (plain) flour
- 1 tablespoon instant espresso powder
- $1\frac{1}{2}$ teaspoons vanilla extract (essence)

White Chocolate Ganache

- 6 ounces (180 g) white chocolate, chopped
- 5 tablespoons (75 ml) heavy (double) cream
- $\frac{1}{4}$ teaspoon ground cinnamon

Brownies Preheat the oven to 325°F (170°C/gas 3). Butter an 8-inch (20-cm) square baking pan. Melt the butter and chocolate in a double boiler over barely simmering water. Remove from the heat and whisk in the sugar. Whisk in the eggs one at a time, followed by the flour, coffee, and vanilla. Pour into the pan.

Bake for 30–35 minutes, until the top is set and a toothpick inserted into center comes out with moist crumbs attached. Cool in the pan on a rack.

White Chocolate Ganache Whisk the chocolate, cream, and cinnamon in a small saucepan over low heat until smooth. Pour evenly over the brownies in the pan. Chill until the ganache is set, at least 2 hours.

MAKES 12–16 • PREPARATION 20 MIN. + 2 HR. TO CHILL • COOKING 30–35 MIN. • LEVEL 1

6 mocha & pecan brownies

Brownies
- 2 cups (400 g) sugar
- 3/4 cup (180 g) salted butter
- 3/4 cup (120 g) unsweetened cocoa powder
- 3 tablespoons finely ground coffee beans
- 3 large eggs
- 1 1/2 teaspoons vanilla extract (essence)
- 1 1/3 cups (200 g) all-purpose (plain) flour
- 3/4 cup (100 g) pecan pieces

Frosting
- 1 cup (180 g) dark chocolate chips
- 6 tablespoons (90 ml) freshly brewed strong black coffee

Brownies Preheat the oven to 350°F (180°C/gas 4). Butter a 9 x 13-inch (23 x 33-cm) pan.

Combine the sugar, butter, cocoa, and ground coffee in a double boiler over barely simmering water and whisk until the butter melts. The texture will be grainy. Set aside and let cool to lukewarm. Whisk in the eggs and vanilla, followed by the flour. Stir in the pecans.

Spoon the batter into the prepared pan. Bake for 25–30 minutes, until the top is set and a toothpick inserted into center comes out with just a few moist crumbs attached. Cool in the pan on a rack.

Frosting Put the chocolate chips in small bowl. Bring the coffee to a simmer in a small saucepan over medium heat. Pour over the chocolate chips and stir until melted and smooth. Let stand until cool and beginning to thicken, about one hour. Spread evenly over the brownies.

MAKES 20–24 • PREPARATION 20 MIN. + 1 HR. TO COOL • COOKING 25–30 MIN. • LEVEL 1

This recipe makes a large pan of delicious brownies. Mocha and pecan is a classic combo, but walnuts and almonds will also work well.

7 chocolate coconut cupcakes

Cupcakes
- 3 ounces (90 g) dark chocolate, chopped
- ⅔ cup (150 ml) light (single) cream
- ⅔ cup (100 g) self-raising flour
- ½ cup (60 g) shredded (desiccated) coconut

2 tablespoons unsweetened cocoa powder
- ⅓ cup (90 g) salted butter, softened
- 1 cup (200 g) sugar
- 2 large eggs

Chocolate Ganache
- 2 ounces (60 g) dark chocolate, coarsely chopped
- ½ cup (125 ml) light (single) cream
- 2 tablespoons shredded (desiccated) coconut

Cupcakes Preheat the oven to 325°F (170°C/gas 3). Line a standard 12-cup muffin tin with paper liners. Melt the chocolate with the cream in a double boiler over barely simmering water. Mix the flour, coconut, and cocoa in a bowl. Beat the butter and sugar until pale and creamy. Beat in the eggs. Beat in the flour and chocolate mixtures. Spoon into the prepared cups. Bake for 25–30 minutes, until golden brown and firm to the touch. Let cool on a rack.

Chocolate Ganache Melt the chocolate with the cream in a double boiler over barely simmering water. Chill for 20 minutes until thickened. Spread on the cupcakes and top with the coconut.

MAKES 12 • PREPARATION 25 MIN. + 20 MIN. TO CHILL • COOKING 25–30 MIN. • LEVEL 1

8 marbled chocolate cupcakes

Chocolate Mixture
- ½ cup (120 g) salted butter, cut into 3 pieces
- 4 ounces (120 g) dark chocolate, coarsely chopped
- 4 large eggs
- 2 cups (400 g) sugar
- 1 teaspoon vanilla extract (essence)
- 1⅓ cups (200 g) all-purpose (plain) flour
- 1 teaspoon baking powder

Cream Cheese Mixture
- 6 ounces (180 g) cream cheese, softened
- 3 tablespoons sugar
- 1 large egg yolk
- ½ cup (90 g) dark chocolate chips

Chocolate Mixture Preheat the oven to 350°F (180°C/gas 4). Line a standard 12-cup muffin tin with paper liners. Melt the butter and chocolate in a double boiler over barely simmering water. Beat the eggs and sugar until thick and pale. Fold in the chocolate mixture and vanilla, followed by the flour and baking powder.

Cream Cheese Mixture Beat the cream cheese and sugar until smooth and creamy. Add the egg yolk and mix until blended. Stir in the chocolate chips.

Put alternate spoonfuls of the mixtures into the cups. Bake for 20–25 minutes, until risen. Let cool on a rack.

MAKES 12 • PREPARATION 20 MIN. • COOKING 20–25 MIN. • LEVEL 2

9 chocolate mint cupcakes

Cupcakes
- 2 cups (300 g) all-purpose (plain) flour
- ½ cup (75 g) unsweetened cocoa powder
- 1 teaspoon baking powder
- ½ teaspoon baking soda (bicarbonate of soda)
- ⅔ cup (150 g) salted butter, softened
- 1½ cups (300 g) sugar
- 3 large eggs
- ¾ cup (180 ml) milk
- 1 teaspoon peppermint extract
- 12 chocolate cream after-dinner mints (After Eights), chopped

Chocolate Glaze
- 6 ounces (180 g) dark chocolate, coarsely chopped
- ½ cup (120 g) salted butter, cut up
- 1 teaspoon peppermint extract

Cupcakes Preheat the oven to 350°F (180°C/gas 4). Line 18 muffin cups with aluminum foil or paper liners. Mix the flour, cocoa, baking powder, and baking soda in a large bowl. Beat the butter and sugar in a large bowl with an electric mixer at medium speed until pale and creamy. Add the eggs one at a time, until just blended after each addition. With the mixer on low speed, beat in the dry ingredients, alternating with the milk and peppermint extract. Stir in the chocolate mints. Spoon the batter into the prepared cups. Bake for 20–30 minutes, until a toothpick inserted into the center comes out clean. Cool the cupcakes on a wire rack.

Chocolate Glaze Melt the chocolate and butter in a double boiler over barely simmering water. Add the peppermint extract. Set aside to cool a little and thicken. Drizzle on the cupcakes.

MAKES 18 • PREPARATION 30 MIN. • COOKING 20–30 MIN. • LEVEL 1

Chocolate and peppermint are a classic combination and work especially well in these rich little cakes. Serve for dessert with tiny cups of strong espresso coffee. For special occasions, dress them up by removing the paper liners and wrapping each cupcake in colored paper.

10 chocolate meringues

Meringues
- 4 ounces (120 g) dark chocolate
- 3 large egg whites
- 3/4 cup (150 g) superfine (caster) sugar

Filling
- 2 tablespoons unsweetened cocoa powder
- 1/3 cup (50 g) confectioners' (icing) sugar
- 2 tablespoons boiling water
- 3/4 cup (180 ml) heavy (double) double cream
- 2 ounces (60 g) dark chocolate, to decorate

Meringues Preheat the oven to 300°F (150°C/gas 2). Line two large baking sheets with parchment paper. Melt the chocolate in a double boiler over barely simmering water. Beat the egg whites with an electric mixer on medium speed until frothy. Gradually beat in the sugar until thick and glossy. Gently fold in the chocolate to create a rippled effect. Spoon 24 even-size meringues onto the baking sheets, spacing well. Bake for 30 minutes. Turn off the oven. Let dry out overnight.

Filling Mix the cocoa, confectioners' sugar, and boiling water in a small bowl until smooth. Beat the cream until stiff. Fold in the cocoa mixture. Sandwich the meringues together with the filling. Melt the chocolate in a double boiler. Pipe chocolate over each meringue.

MAKES 12 • PREPARATION 30 MIN. + 12 HR. TO DRY OUT • COOKING 30 MIN. • LEVEL 2

11 florentines

- $^{1}/_{2}$ cup (125 g) salted butter
- $^{3}/_{4}$ cup (150 g) sugar
- 2 teaspoons honey
- $^{1}/_{2}$ cup (50 g) flaked almonds, toasted
- $^{2}/_{3}$ cup (70 g) finely chopped dried cranberries
- $^{2}/_{3}$ cup (70 g) finely chopped dried pineapple
- $^{2}/_{3}$ cup (70 g) finely chopped dried apricots
- $^{3}/_{4}$ cup (125 g) all-purpose (plain) flour
- 5 ounces (150 g) dark chocolate, coarsely chopped

Preheat the oven to 350°F (180°C/gas 4). Line four baking sheets with parchment paper. Melt the butter, sugar, and honey over low heat until the sugar has dissolved. Increase the heat and bring almost to a boil. Remove from the heat and mix in the almonds and dried fruit. Add the flour and stir until well blended.

Drop teaspoons of dough 3 inches (8 cm) apart onto the baking sheets. Bake for 8–10 minutes, until golden brown. Cool on the sheets until slightly firm. Cool completely on racks. Melt the chocolate in a double boiler. Brush one side of each cookie with the chocolate and let stand until set, about 30 minutes.

MAKES 40–45 • PREPARATION 25 MIN. + 30 MIN. TO STAND • COOKING 8–10 MIN. • LEVEL 2

12 chocolate macaroons

Macaroons
- 1 cup (150 g) confectioners' (icing) sugar
- 1 tablespoon unsweetened cocoa powder
- $\frac{2}{3}$ cup (100 g) finely ground almonds
- 2 large egg whites

Filling
- 3 ounces (90 g) dark chocolate, chopped
- 1 tablespoon milk, warmed

Macaroons Line three large baking sheets with parchment paper. Sift the confectioners' sugar and cocoa into a bowl. Stir in the ground almonds.

Beat the egg whites in a medium bowl with an electric mixer on medium speed until stiff and dry. Add half the almond and cocoa mixture to the meringue and use a large metal spoon to fold it in. Fold in the remaining almond and cocoa mixture. Transfer to a piping bag and pipe out 24–30 small circles about 1½ inches (3–4 cm) in diameter on the baking sheets, spacing 1 inch (2.5 cm) apart.

Put the baking sheets in a cool dry place and let rest for 30 minutes. The macaroons will harden slightly and will not stick to your finger if you poke them lightly.

Preheat the oven to 350°F (180°C/gas 4). Bake the macaroons for 15–20 minutes, until risen and smooth on top. If they begin to split, crack your oven door open a fraction to cool it down slightly. Remove from the oven and let cool completely on the baking sheets.

Filling Melt the chocolate in a double boiler over barely simmering water or in the microwave. Stir in the milk until smooth. Leave to cool and thicken, about 15 minutes. Sandwich the macaroons together in pairs with the filling.

MAKES 12–15 • PREPARATION 20 MIN. + 30 MIN. TO REST • COOKING 40 MIN. • LEVEL 2

13 chocolate caramel tart

Crust
- 1 recipe shortcrust pastry (see page 106)

Caramel Filling
- 1 cup (200 g) sugar
- 1/4 cup (60 ml) water
- 1/4 cup (60 ml) heavy (double) cream
- 1/4 cup (60 g) butter
- 1/2 vanilla bean, split lengthwise
- 1/4 teaspoon salt

Chocolate Ganache
- 1 cup (250 ml) heavy (double) cream
- 6 ounces (200 g) bittersweet chocolate, chopped

Crust Prepare the pastry and pre-bake the crust following the instructions on page 106.

Caramel Filling Combine the sugar and water in a medium saucepan over medium-low heat and stir until the sugar dissolves. Increase the heat to high and boil without stirring until deep amber, about 7 minutes. Remove from the heat and add the cream. Stir in the butter over low heat until completely smooth. Scrape in the vanilla seeds. Stir in the salt. Cool for 10 minutes. Pour into the crust. Let stand until cool, about 1 hour.

Chocolate Ganache Bring the cream to a simmer. Remove from the heat and stir in the chocolate until smooth. Let stand for 10 minutes. Pour over the caramel filling. Refrigerate until firm, about 2 hours.

SERVES 8–12 • PREPARATION 1 HR. + 3 HR. TO COOL & TIME FOR THE CRUST • COOKING 30 MIN. • LEVEL 2

14 bittersweet chocolate tart

Crust
- 1 recipe shortcrust pastry (see page 106)

Filling
- 8 ounces (250 g) bittersweet chocolate, finely chopped
- 5 tablespoons (75 g) butter, cut up
- 1 teaspoon finely grated untreated orange zest
- 1 large egg yolk
- 1/4 cup (60 ml) boiling water
- 1/2 cup (120 ml) heavy (double) cream, whipped
- Candied orange peel

Crust Prepare the pastry and pre-bake the crust following the instructions on page 106.

Filling Melt the chocolate, butter, and orange zest in a double boiler over barely simmering water. Whisk the egg yolk with the boiling water. Stir into the chocolate mixture until smooth. Simmer in the double boiler for 3 minutes. Pour the chocolate filling into the crust. Cover and chill overnight.

Remove the pan sides. Place the tart on a platter. Fill a pastry bag fitted with a star tip and pipe cream rosettes around edge of the tart. Garnish with candied peel.

SERVES 8–12 • PREPARATION 45 MIN. + 12 HR. TO CHILL • COOKING 30 MIN. • LEVEL 3

15 chocolate cranberry tart

Cranberry Topping
- ½ cup (120 ml) cranberry juice
- 1 teaspoon unflavored gelatin
- 2 cups (300 g) fresh or frozen cranberries
- ¾ cup (150 g) sugar
- 2 teaspoons freshly squeezed lemon juice
- 1 teaspoon finely grated untreated lemon zest
- 1 teaspoon finely grated fresh ginger
- Pinch of salt
- 4 tablespoons finely chopped candied crystallized ginger

Crust
- 1¼ cups (200 g) chocolate wafer cookie crumbs
- ¼ cup (50 g) sugar
- ⅓ cup (90 g) salted butter, melted

Mascarpone Filling
- 8 ounces (250 g) mascarpone cheese
- ½ cup (75 g) confectioners' (icing) sugar
- ½ cup (120 ml) chilled heavy (double) cream
- 1 teaspoon vanilla extract (essence)

Cranberry Topping Pour half the cranberry juice into a small bowl and sprinkle with the gelatin. Let stand until softened, 15 minutes. Combine the remaining cranberry juice, cranberries, sugar, lemon juice, lemon zest, ginger, and salt in a medium saucepan. Bring to a boil, stirring until the sugar dissolves. Reduce the heat to medium and simmer until the cranberries are just tender, about 5 minutes. Strain into a bowl and set aside.

Add the gelatin mixture to the hot juice in the bowl. Stir until the gelatin dissolves. Stir cranberries back into juice. Chill overnight. Stir the candied ginger into cranberry mixture.

Crust Preheat the oven to 350°F (180°C/gas 4). Combine the cookie crumbs and sugar in a bowl. Stir in the butter. Press the crumb mixture firmly into the bottom and up the sides of a 9-inch (23-cm) tart pan with a removable bottom. Bake the crust for 15 minutes, until slightly crisp. Place on a rack and let cool completely before filling.

Filling Beat all the ingredients in a medium bowl until thick enough to spread. Spread the filling into the cooled crust. Spoon the cranberry mixture evenly over the filling. Chill for 6 hours before serving.

SERVES 8–12 • PREPARATION 1 HR. + 18 HR. TO CHILL • COOKING 45 MIN. • LEVEL 3

16 chocolate layer cake

Cake
- 2 cups (300 g) all-purpose (plain) flour
- $1\frac{3}{4}$ cups (350 g) sugar
- $\frac{3}{4}$ cup (120 g) unsweetened cocoa powder
- 2 teaspoons baking soda (bicarbonate of soda)
- $\frac{1}{4}$ teaspoon salt
- 1 cup (250 ml) water
- $\frac{3}{4}$ cup (180 ml) buttermilk
- $\frac{3}{4}$ cup (180 ml) vegetable oil
- 3 large eggs

Filling & Topping
- $1\frac{1}{4}$ pounds (600 g) bittersweet chocolate, chopped
- $2\frac{1}{4}$ cups (600 ml) heavy (double) cream
- 6 tablespoons seedless raspberry preserves (jam)

Cake Preheat the oven to 350°F (180°C/gas 4). Butter two 9-inch (23-cm) cake pans. Mix the flour, sugar, cocoa, baking soda, and salt in a bowl. Whisk the water, buttermilk, oil, and eggs in a bowl. Whisk the water mixture into the dry ingredients. Spoon into the pans. Bake for 30–35 minutes, until a toothpick inserted into the center comes out clean. Cool on wire racks.

Filling & Topping Put the chocolate in a bowl. Bring the cream to a boil and pour over the chocolate. Stir until smooth. Transfer $1\frac{1}{4}$ cups to a small bowl and chill for 1 hour. Put one cake on a platter. Spread with half the raspberry preserves. Spread with the chilled ganache. Cover with the other cake and spread with the remaining jam. Pour the remaining ganache over the top. Freeze until set, about 30 minutes.

SERVES 12 • PREPARATION 30 MIN. + $1\frac{1}{2}$ HR. TO CHILL • COOKING 30–35 MIN. • LEVEL 2

17 chocolate beet cake

Cake

- 8 ounces (250 g) dark chocolate, broken up
- 3 large eggs
- 1 cup (200 g) firmly packed light brown sugar
- 1/3 cup (90 ml) sunflower oil
- 1 teaspoon vanilla extract
- 2/3 cup (100 g) all-purpose (plain) flour
- 1 teaspoon baking powder
- 1/2 teaspoon baking soda (bicarbonate of soda)
- 1/3 cup (50 g) finely ground almonds
- 8 ounces (250 g) raw beetroot, peeled and grated

Frosting

- 5 ounces (150 g) dark chocolate
- 1 cup (150 g) confectioners' (icing) sugar
- 1/3 cup (90 ml) sour cream

Preheat the oven to 350°F (180°C/gas 4). Grease a 9-inch (23-cm) springform pan with butter. Melt the chocolate in a double boiler over barely simmering water. Set aside to cool.

Whisk the eggs, sugar, and oil in a large bowl until smooth. Stir in the vanilla, then fold in the flour, baking powder, baking soda, and ground almonds. Squeeze the excess liquid out of the beets then fold into the batter. Spoon into the prepared pan. Bake for 50–60 minutes, until a toothpick inserted into the center comes out clean. Cool on a wire rack.

Frosting Melt the chocolate in a double boiler. Remove from the heat and beat in the confectioners' sugar and sour cream. Spread over the top and sides of the cake.

SERVES 8 • PREPARATION 15–20 MIN. • COOKING 25–35 MIN. • LEVEL 1

18 chocolate mayonnaise cake

Cake

- 2 ounces (60 g) dark chocolate, chopped
- $\frac{2}{3}$ cup (100 g) unsweetened cocoa powder
- $1\frac{3}{4}$ cups (430 ml) boiling water
- 3 cups (450 g) all-purpose (plain) flour
- $1\frac{1}{4}$ teaspoons baking soda (bicarbonate of soda)
- $\frac{1}{4}$ teaspoon baking powder
- 1 cup (200 g) sugar
- 1 cup (200 g) firmly packed dark brown sugar
- $1\frac{1}{3}$ cups (300 ml) full-fat mayonnaise
- 2 large eggs
- 1 teaspoon vanilla extract (essence)

Chocolate Frosting

- 12 ounces (350 g) dark chocolate, chopped
- $1\frac{1}{2}$ cups (375 g) unsalted butter
- 3 cups (450 g) confectioners' (icing) sugar
- 1 tablespoon vanilla extract (essence)
- Chocolate curls, to decorate

Cake Preheat the oven to 350°F (180°C/gas 4). Butter and flour three 8-inch (20-cm) cake pans. Combine the chocolate and cocoa in a medium metal bowl. Add the boiling water and whisk until the chocolate is melted.

Combine the flour, baking soda, and baking powder in a medium bowl. Beat both sugars and the mayonnaise in a large bowl until well blended, 2–3 minutes. Add the eggs one at a time, beating until just blended after each addition. Beat in the vanilla. With the mixer on low speed, gradually beat in the flour mixture alternately with the chocolate mixture. Divide the batter evenly among the prepared cake pans.

Bake the cakes for 30–35 minutes, until a toothpick inserted into the center comes out clean. Cool in the pans on racks for 30 minutes. Carefully invert the cakes onto racks and let cool completely.

Chocolate Frosting Melt the chocolate in a double boiler over barely simmering water. Set aside. Beat the butter and confectioners' sugar until creamy. Beat in the vanilla. Add the chocolate and beat until smooth.

Place one cake layer on a platter. Spread with $\frac{3}{4}$ cup of frosting. Top with a second cake layer and spread with $\frac{3}{4}$ cup of frosting. Top with the third cake layer. Spread the remaining frosting over the top and sides. Top with the chocolate curls.

SERVES 12 • PREPARATION 45 MIN. • COOKING 30–35 MIN. • LEVEL 2

19 marbled cheesecake

Crust

- $1\frac{1}{2}$ cups (200 g) plain chocolate wafer (biscuit) crumbs
- $\frac{1}{3}$ cup (30 g) ground hazelnuts
- $\frac{1}{2}$ cup (120 g) salted butter, melted

Filling

- 2 teaspoons unflavored powdered gelatin
- 4 tablespoons (60 ml) water
- 5 ounces (150 g) dark chocolate
- 1 pound (500 g) cream cheese, softened
- $\frac{1}{3}$ cup (50 g) confectioners' (icing) sugar
- 2 tablespoons hazelnuts, toasted and finely chopped
- 2 tablespoons hazelnut liqueur, such as Frangelico
- 1 cup (250 ml) light (single) cream

Crust Combine the crumbs, hazelnuts, and butter in a small bowl. Press into the bottom of a 10-inch (25-cm) springform pan. Refrigerate for 1 hour.

Filling Sprinkle the gelatin over the water in a small bowl, stirring until dissolved. Melt the chocolate in a double boiler over barely simmering water until smooth.

Beat the cream cheese and confectioners' sugar until smooth. Beat in the gelatin mixture. Divide evenly between two bowls. Add the chocolate to one bowl and the hazelnuts and liqueur to the other. Whip the cream until soft peaks form. Divide in half and fold into the chocolate and hazelnut mixtures. Pour alternately into the prepared base. Refrigerate for 6 hours.

SERVES 8–12 • PREPARATION 45 MIN. + 7 HR. TO CHILL • LEVEL 2

20 chocolate whiskey cake

Cake
- $\frac{1}{2}$ cup (120 ml) whiskey
- 6 ounces (180 g) bittersweet chocolate, chopped
- 2 teaspoons instant coffee dissolved in 6 tablespoons (90 ml) boiling water
- $\frac{1}{2}$ cup (120 g) salted butter
- 6 tablespoons vanilla sugar
- 3 large eggs, separated
- $\frac{1}{2}$ cup (75 g) finely ground almonds
- 4 tablespoons all-purpose (plain) flour, divided

Frosting
- 4 ounces (120 g) dark chocolate, chopped
- 2 tablespoons whiskey
- $\frac{1}{4}$ cup (60 g) salted butter
- Fresh blueberries, to decorate

Cake Preheat the oven to 350°F (180°C/gas 4). Butter an 8-inch (20-cm) springform pan. Simmer the whiskey in saucepan until reduced by half, 2–3 minutes. Mix the chocolate, coffee mixture, and whiskey in a double boiler. Stir over barely simmering water until smooth.

Beat the butter and vanilla sugar until creamy. Beat in the egg yolks. Fold in the chocolate mixture and almonds. Beat the egg whites until stiff peaks form. Fold into the batter alternately with the flour. Spoon into the pan. Bake for 35–40 minutes, until firm.

Frosting Stir the chocolate and whiskey in double boiler over barely simmering water until smooth. Remove from the heat and beat in the butter. Spread over the cake and decorate with the blueberries.

SERVES 8–12 • PREPARATION 30 MIN. • COOKING 35–30 MIN. • LEVEL 2

1
vanilla hearts

2
cat face cookies

3
lemon meringue cookies

4
tropical morning muffins

5
black cat cupcakes

6
mother's day cupcakes

7
birthday cupcakes

8
vanilla cupcakes
with orange & lemon frosting

9
filo, berries & cream

10
chocolate meringues
with honeycomb chocolate

11
meringues with rose cream

12
cheesecake tart with berry topping

13
orange ricotta tart

14
chocolate pecan tart

special occasions

15
chocolate meringue pie

16
chocolate cake with chantilly cream

17
golden layer cake

18
spiced pumpkin layer cake

19
chocolate cream roulade

20
coffee cream roulade

1 vanilla hearts

Cookies
- $1\frac{1}{2}$ cups (225 g) all-purpose (plain) flour
- $\frac{1}{3}$ cup (75 g) superfine (caster) sugar
- $\frac{2}{3}$ cup (150 g) salted butter, chilled and cut up

Frosting
- $1\frac{1}{2}$ cups (225 g) confectioners' (icing) sugar
- $\frac{1}{2}$ teaspoon vanilla extract (essence)
- 1 tablespoon hot milk
- Tiny sugar roses, to decorate

Cookies Combine the flour and sugar in a bowl. Rub in the butter then bring together in a ball. Wrap in plastic wrap (cling film) and chill for 30 minutes.

Preheat the oven to 350°F (180°C/gas 4). Line two baking sheets with parchment paper. Roll the dough out on a floured work surface to ⅛ inch (3 mm) thick. Use a heart-shaped cookie cutter to cut out cookies. Gather the dough scraps, re-roll, and continue until all the dough is used. Transfer to the baking sheets. Bake for 12–15 minutes, until pale golden brown. Let cool on the baking sheets until they harden a little, 2–3 minutes. Transfer to racks and let cool completely.

Frosting Combine the confectioners' sugar in a bowl with the vanilla and milk and stir to make a smooth paste. Spread over the cookies. Press a sugar rose into the top of each cookie. Leave to set for 30 minutes.

SERVES 15–25 • PREPARATION 30 MIN. + 1 HR. TO CHILL & SET • COOKING 12–15 MIN. • LEVEL 2

2 cat face cookies

- 2 tablespoons salted butter, softened
- $\frac{1}{4}$ cup (50 g) sugar
- 1 tablespoon honey
- 3 tablespoons all-purpose (plain) flour
- 1 tablespoon unsweetened cocoa powder
- 1 large egg white
- $\frac{1}{4}$ teaspoon rum extract (essence)
- $\frac{1}{4}$ teaspoon vanilla extract (essence)
- $\frac{1}{4}$ cup (45 g) dark chocolate chips

Beat the butter and sugar in a large bowl with an electric mixer on medium speed until pale and creamy. Beat in the honey, flour, cocoa, and egg white. Add the rum and vanilla extracts. Chill for 1–2 hours.

Preheat the oven to 325°F (170°C/gas 3). Line three baking sheets with parchment paper. Draw the outline of a cat's head (about 3 inches/8 cm in diameter) on a square of acetate or thick plastic. Cut out to make a stencil. Place the stencil on the paper at the top corner of the baking sheet. Spread with a thin layer of cookie dough. Carefully lift the stencil and place on the paper next to the cat face you just made, spacing 2 inches (5 cm) apart. Repeat until all the dough is used. Bake for 8–10 minutes, until just firm. Decorate with chocolate chips to make eyes and noses. Transfer to racks to cool.

MAKES 20–24 • PREPARATION 30 MIN. + 1–2 HR TO CHILL • COOKING 8–10 MIN. • LEVEL 2

3 lemon meringue cookies

Meringues
- $^1/_4$ cup (50 g) sugar
- $^2/_3$ cup (100 g) confectioners' (icing) sugar
- $^1/_8$ teaspoon salt
- 2 large egg whites
- $^1/_4$ teaspoon cream of tartar
- $^1/_2$ teaspoon vanilla extract (essence)
- $^1/_2$ teaspoon pure lemon extract (essence)
- 4–6 finely crushed gingersnap (gingernut) or amaretti cookies

Lemon Curd
- $^1/_2$ cup (120 g) salted butter
- $^3/_4$ cup (150 g) sugar
- $^1/_2$ cup (120 ml) freshly squeezed lemon juice
- 3 tablespoons lightly packed finely grated untreated lemon zest
- 6 large egg yolks

Meringues Preheat the oven to 175°F (80°C). Line two baking sheets with parchment paper. Combine the sugar, confectioners' sugar, and salt in a bowl. Beat the egg whites and cream of tartar with an electric mixer on medium speed until frothy. Gradually add the sugar mixture and beat until firm, glossy peaks form. Beat in the vanilla and lemon extracts.

Spoon the meringue into a pastry bag fitted with a plain $^1/_2$-inch (1-cm) tip. Pipe 1$^1/_4$ inch (3–4 cm) disks onto the baking sheets, spacing well. Sprinkle with the crushed cookies. Bake for 2 hours, until dried and crisp. Turn off the oven and let the meringues sit inside until cool, about 2 hours. Remove from the oven and gently lift the meringues off the parchment paper.

Lemon Curd Melt the butter in a saucepan over medium heat. Remove the pan from the heat and whisk in the sugar, and lemon juice and zest. Whisk in the egg yolks. Return the pan to low heat and cook, whisking constantly, until thickened, 5–6 minutes. Don't let the mixture boil. Force the curd through a fine-metal sieve into a bowl. Let cool to room temperature, whisking occasionally. Chill until ready to use.

Sandwich the meringues together with the lemon curd and serve.

MAKES 20–24 • PREPARATION 30 MIN. + 2 HR. TO COOL • COOKING 2 HR. • LEVEL 2

4 tropical morning muffins

Cupcakes
- 2 cups (300 g) all-purpose (plain) flour
- 2 teaspoons baking powder
- $^1/_2$ teaspoon baking soda (bicarbonate of soda)
- $^1/_2$ cup (120 g) salted butter, softened
- $^3/_4$ cup (150 g) sugar
- 2 large eggs
- $^1/_2$ cup (120 ml) heavy (double) cream
- $^1/_2$ cup (70 g) finely chopped candied (glacé) mango
- $^1/_4$ cup (60 ml) fresh passion fruit pulp

Yogurt Filling
- $^1/_2$ cup (120 mm) heavy (double) cream
- $^1/_2$ cup (120 ml) plain yogurt
- 2 teaspoons finely grated untreated lemon zest

Cupcakes Preheat the oven to 350°F (180°C/gas 4). Line a 12-cup muffin tin with paper liners. Mix the flour, baking powder, and baking soda in a bowl. Beat the butter and sugar in a bowl with an electric mixer on medium speed until pale and creamy. Add the eggs one at a time, beating until just blended after each addition. With the mixer on low speed, beat in the flour mixture, cream, mango, and passion fruit. Spoon the batter into the prepared cups. Bake for 15–20 minutes, until risen and golden. Cool the muffins on racks.

Yogurt Filling Beat the cream and yogurt in a medium bowl until stiff. Fold in the lemon zest. Cut the top off each muffin. Fill with yogurt cream and cover with the muffin tops.

MAKES 12 • PREPARATION 30 MIN. • COOKING 15–20 MIN. • LEVEL 1

5 black cat cupcakes

Cupcakes

- $^3/_4$ cup (125 g) all-purpose (plain) flour
- 3 tablespoons unsweetened cocoa powder
- 1 teaspoon baking powder
- $^1/_2$ cup (125 g) salted butter, softened
- $^3/_4$ cup (150 g) firmly packed dark brown sugar
- $^1/_2$ teaspoon vanilla extract (essence)
- 2 large eggs
- 3 tablespoons milk

To Decorate

- $1^1/_2$ cups (225 g) confectioners' (icing) sugar
- 2 tablespoons water
- Yellow food coloring
- 12 confectionery black cats

Cupcakes Preheat the oven to 325°F (170°C/gas 3). Line a standard 12-cup muffin tin with paper liners. Combine the flour, cocoa, and baking powder in a bowl. Beat the butter, sugar, and vanilla in a medium bowl with an electric mixer on medium speed until creamy. Add the eggs one at a time, beating until just blended after each addition. With the mixer on low speed, gradually add the flour mixture, alternating with the milk. Spoon the batter into the prepared cups. Bake for 20–25 minutes, until golden brown. Transfer to a wire rack. Let cool completely.

To Decorate Stir the confectioners' sugar, water, and food coloring in a bowl to make a yellow frosting. Spread over the cupcakes and top with the cats.

MAKES 12 • PREPARATION 30 MIN. • COOKING 15–20 MIN. • LEVEL 1

6 mother's day cupcakes

Cupcakes
- 2 cups (300 g) all-purpose (plain) flour
- 1 teaspoon baking powder
- 1/2 teaspoon baking soda (bicarbonate of soda)
- 1 teaspoon ground cinnamon
- 1/4 teaspoon ground cloves
- 1/4 teaspoon salt
- 2 large eggs
- 3/4 cup (150 g) sugar
- 1/2 cup (120 ml) vegetable oil
- 1/4 cup (60 ml) water
- 3/4 cup (135 g) tart apple, such as Granny Smiths, peeled, cored, and finely chopped
- 1/2 cup (60 g) walnuts, coarsely chopped

Cream Cheese Frosting
- 5 ounces (150 g) cream cheese, softened
- 1/2 teaspoon finely grated untreated lemon zest
- 2/3 cup (100 g) confectioners' (icing) sugar
- 1 tablespoon freshly squeezed lemon juice, strained
- Sugar flowers, to decorate

Cupcakes Preheat the oven to 325°F (170°C/gas 3). Line a standard 12-cup muffin tin with paper liners. Combine the flour, baking powder, baking soda, cinnamon, cloves, and salt in a medium bowl. Beat the eggs in a medium bowl with an electric mixer on medium speed until frothy. Add the sugar, oil, and water and beat until incorporated. With the mixer on low speed, gradually add the flour mixture. Stir in the apple and walnuts by hand.

Spoon the batter into the prepared cups. Bake for 25–30 minutes, until golden brown and firm to the touch. Transfer the muffin tin to a wire rack. Let cool completely before removing the cupcakes.

Cream Cheese Frosting Beat the cream cheese and lemon zest in a small bowl with an electric mixer on medium speed until creamy. Add the confectioners' sugar and lemon juice, beating until combined. Spread some frosting on each cupcake. Decorate with the flowers and serve.

MAKES 12 • PREPARATION 30 MIN. • COOKING 25–30 MIN. • LEVEL 1

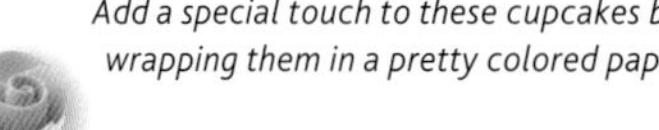

Add a special touch to these cupcakes by wrapping them in a pretty colored paper.

7 birthday cupcakes

Cupcakes
- 2 cups (300 g) ground pecans
- $1\frac{1}{4}$ cups (250 g) sugar
- $\frac{1}{4}$ cup (30 g) unsweetened cocoa powder
- 1 teaspoon baking powder
- 1 teaspoon ground cinnamon
- 4 large eggs
- $\frac{1}{2}$ cup (120 g) salted butter, melted
- 1 teaspoon vanilla extract
- 1 recipe chocolate ganache (see page 130)

To Decorate
- 1 cup (150 g) confectioners' (icing) sugar
- 1 tablespoon boiling water
- Numbered candles

Cupcakes Preheat the oven to 325°F (170°C/gas 3). Line a standard 12-cup muffin tin with paper liners. Combine the pecans, sugar, cocoa, baking powder, and cinnamon in a bowl. Whisk the eggs, butter, and vanilla in a small bowl. Pour the egg mixture into the flour mixture and stir until just combined. Spoon the batter into the prepared cups. Bake for 30–35 minutes, until firm to the touch. Transfer to a wire rack. Let cool completely, then spread with the chocolate ganache.

To Decorate Stir the confectioners' sugar and water in a small bowl until smooth. Spoon into an envelope. Cut the tip off using scissors. Pipe decorations on the cupcakes. Arrange the candles in one cupcake.

MAKES 12 • PREPARATION 45 MIN. • COOKING 30–35 MIN. • LEVEL 2

8 vanilla cupcakes
with orange & lemon frosting

Cupcakes
- $^{2}/_{3}$ cup (150 g) salted butter, softened
- $^{3}/_{4}$ cup (150 g) sugar
- 2 large eggs
- 1 teaspoon vanilla extract (essence)
- 1 cup (150 g) + 3 tablespoons all-purpose (plain) flour
- $1^{1}/_{2}$ teaspoons baking powder
- 2 tablespoons milk

Frosting
- $^{1}/_{3}$ cup (90 g) unsalted butter, softened
- 2 cups (300 g) confectioners' (icing) sugar
- 4 teaspoons freshly squeezed orange juice
- 4 teaspoons freshly squeezed lemon juice

Cupcakes Preheat the oven to 350°F (180°C/gas 4). Line 8 standard muffin cups with paper liners. Beat the butter and sugar in a bowl with an electric mixer on medium speed until pale and creamy. Add the eggs one at a time. Beat in vanilla. With the mixer on low, beat in the flour, baking powder, and milk. Spoon the batter into the cups. Bake for 20–25 minutes, until golden brown. Transfer to a wire rack. Let cool completely.

Frosting Beat the butter and confectioners' sugar in a bowl until smooth. Beat in the orange and lemon juice. Pipe or spread the frosting over the cupcakes.

MAKES 8 • PREPARATION 25 MIN. • COOKING 20–25 MIN. • LEVEL 1

9 filo, berries & cream

- 24 (9 x 14-inch/23 x 35-cm) sheets filo (phyllo) pastry
- 1/3 cup (90 g) unsalted butter, melted
- 16 teaspoons + 1/2 cup (100 g) sugar
- 2/3 cup (150 ml) balsamic vinegar
- 1 pound (500 g) mascarpone cheese, softened
- 1 cup (250 ml) heavy (double) cream, chilled
- 2 teaspoons vanilla extract (essence)
- 2 cups (300 g) strawberries, thinly sliced
- 3 cups (450 g) blueberries

Preheat the oven to 350°F (180°C/gas 4). Line two baking sheets with parchment paper. Place a filo sheet on a work surface. Brush with butter and sprinkle with 1/2 teaspoon sugar. Top with a second filo sheet. Brush with butter and sprinkle with 1/2 teaspoon sugar. Repeat with two more filo sheets, brushing each one with butter and sprinkling with 1/2 teaspoon sugar. Cut the filo stack in half lengthwise, then cut crosswise into thirds, creating six 4-inch (10-cm) squares. Transfer the squares to one of the baking sheets. Repeat with four more filo sheets to create six more squares. Place on the second baking sheet. Bake for 7–8 minutes, until golden brown. Use a spatula to transfer the filo squares to wire racks. Let cool completely. Repeat with the remaining filo, butter, and sugar, to make 36 squares.

Bring the balsamic vinegar and 4 teaspoons of sugar to a boil in a small saucepan. Simmer on low until syrupy and reduced to 1/4 cup (60 ml), 20–25 minutes.

Beat the mascarpone, cream, vanilla, and remaining 1/2 cup (100 g) of sugar in bowl until stiff peaks form. Place 8 filo squares on a work surface. Spread each one with 1 tablespoon of filling. Cover with strawberries and 1 more tablespoon of filling. Repeat until you have eight desserts each with four layers. Top with the remaining fruit and dust with confectioners' sugar. Drizzle the balsamic vinegar mixture around each serving.

MAKES 8 • PREPARATION 1 HR. • COOKING 35–40 MIN. • LEVEL 3

10 chocolate meringues
with honeycomb chocolate

Chocolate Meringues
- 4 large egg whites
- $1\frac{1}{4}$ cups (250 g) superfine (caster) sugar
- 1 teaspoon white vinegar
- 1 teaspoon vanilla extract (essence)
- 1 tablespoon cornstarch (cornflour)
- 2 tablespoons unsweetened cocoa powder

Topping
- $1\frac{1}{2}$ cups (375 ml) heavy (double) cream
- 2 chocolate-coated honeycomb bars, or other chocolate-coated toffee candy bars, coarsely chopped

Chocolate Meringues Preheat the oven to 250°F (130°C/gas ½). Line a large baking sheet with parchment paper. Beat the egg whites in a bowl with an electric mixer on medium speed until frothy. Beat in the sugar until stiff, glossy peaks form. Combine the vinegar, vanilla, cornstarch, and cocoa in a bowl. Fold into the egg whites. Spread six 4-inch (10-cm) meringues on the prepared sheet. Bake for 1 hour, until crisp and dry. Turn the oven off and leave until cooled, about 2 hours.

Topping Beat the cream in a bowl until soft peaks form. Spoon onto the meringues. Pile the honeycomb on top. Serve immediately.

SERVES 6 • PREPARATION 30 MIN. + 2 HR. TO COOL • COOKING 1 HR. • LEVEL 2

11 meringues
with rose cream

Meringues
- 4 large egg whites
- 1 tablespoon confectioners' (icing) sugar
- Pinch of salt
- 1 cup (200 g) sugar
- 1/2 teaspoon vanilla extract (essence)

Filling
- 1 cup (250 ml) heavy (double) cream)
- 2 tablespoons confectioners' (icing) sugar
- 1/2 teaspoon red food coloring

Meringues Preheat the oven to 250°F (130°C/gas 1/2). Line two baking sheets with parchment paper. Beat the egg whites, confectioners' sugar, and salt in a bowl with an electric mixer on medium speed until frothy. Beat in the sugar until stiff, glossy peaks form. Fold in the vanilla. Spoon the meringue into a piping bag with a plain tip and pipe golf ball-size blobs onto the baking sheets, spacing well. Bake for 1 hour, until crisp and dry. Turn off the oven and let cool, about 2 hours.

Filling Beat the cream and confectioners' sugar in a bowl until stiff. Fold in the food coloring. Spread half the meringues with cream and press together in pairs. Serve at once.

SERVES 6–8 • PREPARATION 30 MIN. + 2 HR. TO COOL • COOKING 1 HR. • LEVEL 2

12 cheesecake tart
with berry topping

Crust
- 1 recipe shortcrust pastry (see page 106)
- $\frac{1}{3}$ cup (100 g) apple jelly

Filling
- 1 pound (500 g) cream cheese, softened
- $\frac{3}{4}$ cup (150 g) sugar
- 1 large egg
- 1 teaspoon vanilla extract (essence)
- $\frac{1}{2}$ cup (120 ml) sour cream

Topping
- $\frac{1}{3}$ cup (100 g) apple jelly
- 4 strawberries, hulled and sliced
- 2–3 kiwifruit, peeled and thinly sliced
- $\frac{1}{2}$ cup (75 g) raspberries
- $\frac{1}{2}$ cup (75 g) blueberries

Crust Prepare the pastry and pre-bake the crust following the instructions on page 106. Spread the apple jelly over the warm crust and let cool.

Filling Preheat the oven to 350°F (180°C/gas 4). Beat the cream cheese in a bowl until smooth. Add the sugar and beat until pale and fluffy. Beat in the egg and vanilla. Add the sour cream and beat until just blended. Pour the filling into the crust. Bake for 30–35 minutes, until the filling is almost set. Transfer to a wire rack and let cool completely. Chill until cold, at least 4 hours.

Topping Melt the apple jelly in a small saucepan over low heat. Brush over the filling. Arrange a row of strawberry slices around the outer edge of the tart. Lay the kiwifruit slices over the strawberries, partially overlapping them. Arrange a standing row of raspberries inside the kiwifruit slices. Arrange the blueberries in the center of the tart. The fruit should entirely cover the filling in concentric circles.

SERVES 8–12 • PREPARATION 1 HR. + TIME FOR THE CRUST & 4 HR. TO CHILL • COOKING 60–65 MIN. • LEVEL 3

For best results, serve this tart just after filling and decorating. If you do fill it beforehand, chill in the refrigerator until you serve. Don't chill for more than 3–4 hours though, or the crust will become soggy and unappetizing.

13 orange ricotta tart

Crust
- 1 recipe shortcrust pastry (see page 106)

Filling
- 1 large egg + 1 large egg yolk
- 1 cup (250 g) ricotta cheese, drained
- ½ cup (75 g) confectioners' (icing) sugar
- 2 teaspoons finely grated untreated orange zest
- 1 tablespoon Grand Mariner or orange liqueur
- ½ cup (125 ml) heavy (double) cream + extra, to serve (optional)

Crust Prepare the pastry and pre-bake the crust following the instructions on page 106.

Filling Preheat the oven to 350°F (180°C/gas 4). Combine the egg, egg yolk, ricotta, confectioners' sugar, and orange zest and liqueur in a medium bowl. Whip the cream in a small bowl until soft peaks form. Fold the cream into the ricotta mixture and spoon into the prepared tart crust. Bake for 20 minutes, until golden and set. Let cool, then chill for at least 4 hours. Serve with extra whipped cream, if desired.

SERVES 6–8 • PREPARATION 30 MIN. + TIME FOR THE CRUST & 4 HR. TO CHILL • COOKING 20 MIN. • LEVEL 2

14 chocolate pecan tart

Crust
- 1 recipe shortcrust pastry (see page 106)

Filling
- 4 ounces (120 g) dark chocolate, coarsely chopped
- 1/4 cup (60 g) salted butter, softened
- 3/4 cup (150 g) firmly packed dark brown sugar
- 2/3 cup (150 ml) light corn (golden) syrup
- 3 large eggs, lightly beaten
- 1 teaspoon vanilla extract (essence)
- 2 cups (250 g) pecans, coarsely chopped
- Whipped cream or ice cream, to serve (optional)

Crust Prepare the pastry and pre-bake the crust following the instructions on page 106.

Filling Preheat the oven to 350°F (180°C/gas 4). Stir the chocolate in a double boiler over barely simmering water until melted and smooth. Beat the butter, brown sugar, and corn syrup in a medium bowl with an electric mixer on medium speed until creamy. Add the eggs, vanilla, and chocolate, beating until incorporated. Stir in the pecans by hand. Spoon the filling into the prepared tart crust. Bake for 20–30 minutes, until set. Serve warm with whipped cream or ice cream, if liked.

SERVES 6–8 • PREPARATION 30 MIN. + TIME FOR THE CRUST • COOKING 50–60 MIN. • LEVEL 2

15 chocolate meringue pie

Chocolate Pastry
- 1 cup (150 g) all-purpose (plain) flour
- 1/4 cup (30 g) unsweetened cocoa powder
- 1/2 cup (75 g) confectioners' (icing) sugar
- 3 1/2 ounces (100 g) salted butter, chilled and cubed
- 1 large egg yolk
- 2–3 teaspoons iced water

Filling
- 5 ounces (150 g) dark chocolate, chopped
- 1/4 cup (60 ml) heavy (double) cream
- 1 teaspoon vanilla extract (essence)
- 1/4 cup (60 g) unsalted butter, softened
- 1/3 cup (70 g) sugar
- 4 large egg yolks
- 1 cup (150 g) ground almonds

Meringue
- 3 large egg whites
- 3/4 cup (150 g) sugar

Chocolate Pastry Grease a 10-inch (25-cm) tart pan with a removeable base. Combine the flour, cocoa, confectioners' sugar, and butter in a food processor and pulse until the mixture resembles bread crumbs. Add the egg yolk and 2 teaspoons of water and pulse, adding a little more water if necessary, until the dough comes together. Press into a disk, wrap in plastic wrap (cling film), and chill for 30 minutes. Roll the pastry out on a floured work surface to 1/4 inch (5 mm) thick. Line the pan with the pastry. Cover and chill for 30 minutes.

Preheat the oven to 350°F (180°C/gas 4). Cover the pastry case with parchment paper and fill with baking weights, dried beans, or rice. Bake for 15–20 minutes until just firm. Remove the paper and weights.

Filling Melt the chocolate, cream, and vanilla in a double boiler over barely simmering water. Beat the butter and sugar in a bowl with an electric mixer on medium speed until creamy. Add the egg yolks, chocolate mixture, and almonds. Spread over the pastry and bake for 10 minutes.

Meringue Beat the egg whites in a bowl with an electric mixer on medium speed until frothy. Gradually add the sugar, beating until smooth, glossy peaks form. Spoon the meringue over the filling and bake for 15 minutes, until just golden. Serve at room temperature.

SERVES 6–8 • PREPARATION 45 MIN. + 1 HR. TO CHILL • COOKING 40–45 MIN. • LEVEL 2

16 chocolate cake
with chantilly cream

Cake
- 1 cup (150 g) all-purpose (plain) flour
- 4 tablespoons unsweetened cocoa powder
- 1 teaspoon baking powder
- 1/4 teaspoon salt
- 4 large eggs, separated
- 3/4 cup (150 g) sugar
- 1/4 cup (60 ml) milk
- 1 recipe chocolate ganache (see page 130)

Chantilly Cream
- 2 cups (500 ml) heavy (double) cream
- 2 tablespoons sugar
- 1 teaspoon vanilla extract (essence)

Cake Preheat the oven to 375°F (190°C/gas 5). Butter two 8-inch (20-cm) round cake pans. Line with parchment paper. Sift the flour, cocoa, baking powder, and salt into a bowl. Beat the egg yolks and sugar in a bowl with an electric mixer on medium speed until pale and thick. With the mixer on low speed, beat in the flour mixture and milk. Beat the egg whites until stiff. Fold them into the batter. Spoon the batter into the pans. Bake for 25–30 minutes, until springy to the touch. Cool in the pans for 5 minutes. Turn out onto racks. Remove the paper and let cool completely.

Chantilly Cream Beat the cream, sugar, and vanilla until thick. Place one cake on a serving plate and spread with the chantilly. Top with the remaining cake. Spread the top and sides with the ganache.

SERVES 8 • PREPARATION 30 MIN. • COOKING 25–30 MIN. • LEVEL 2

17 golden layer cake

Cake
- $2\frac{2}{3}$ cups (400 g) all-purpose (plain) flour
- 1 teaspoon baking soda (bicarbonate of soda)
- 1 cup (250 g) salted butter
- 2 cups (400 g) sugar
- 2 teaspoons vanilla extract (essence)
- 6 large eggs
- 1 cup (250 ml) sour cream

Golden Frosting
- $\frac{1}{2}$ cup (125 g) salted butter
- 1 cup (200 g) firmly packed light brown sugar
- $\frac{3}{4}$ cup (200 ml) milk
- 2 teaspoons vanilla extract (essence)
- 3 cups (450 g) confectioners' (icing) sugar

Cake Preheat the oven to 350°F (180°C/gas 4). Butter and flour three 9-inch (23-cm) round cake pans. Sift the flour and baking soda into a bowl. Beat the butter, sugar, and vanilla in a bowl until creamy. Add the eggs one at a time, beating until just blended after each addition. Beat in the flour mixture and sour cream. Spoon the batter into the pans. Bake for 20–25 minutes, until a toothpick inserted into the center comes out clean. Cool in the pans for 5 minutes. Turn out onto racks and let cool completely.

Golden Frosting Melt the butter in a saucepan over low heat. Add the brown sugar and milk and simmer for 5 minutes, stirring constantly. Remove from the heat and stir in the vanilla. Beat in the confectioners' sugar until smooth. Place one cake on a serving plate and spread with frosting. Top with another cake and spread with frosting. Top with the remaining cake. Spread the top and sides of the cake with the remaining frosting.

SERVES 8–12 • PREPARATION 45 MIN. • COOKING 20–25 MIN. • LEVEL 2

18 spiced pumpkin layer cake

Cake
- 3 cups (450 g) all-purpose (plain) flour
- 2 teaspoons baking powder
- 1 teaspoon baking soda (bicarbonate of soda)
- 1 tablespoon ground cinnamon
- 2 teaspoons ground ginger
- 1¾ teaspoons ground pumpkin pie spice (allspice)
- 1 teaspoon salt
- ½ teaspoon ground nutmeg
- 1½ cups (300 g) sugar
- 1 cup (200 g) firmly packed dark brown sugar
- 1 cup (250 ml) canola oil
- 4 large eggs
- 1 (15-ounce/400-g) can pumpkin purée
- 1 tablespoon vanilla extract (essence)
- 1 tablespoon finely grated untreated orange zest
- ¾ cup (100 g) raisins
- ¾ cup (100 g) flaked coconut + extra to garnish

Cream Cheese Frosting
- 8 ounces (250 g) cream cheese, softened
- ⅔ cup (150 g) salted butter, softened
- 1 tablespoon dark rum
- 1 teaspoon vanilla extract
- 4 cups (600 g) confectioners' (icing) sugar

Cake Preheat the oven to 350°F (180°C/gas 4). Butter two 9-inch (23-cm) cake pans. Line with parchment paper. Combine the flour, baking powder, baking soda, cinnamon, ginger, pumpkin pie spice, salt, and nutmeg in a bowl. Beat both sugars and the oil in a bowl with an electric mixer on medium speed until just combined. Add the eggs one at a time, beating until just blended after each addition. With the mixer on low speed, add the pumpkin, vanilla, orange zest, and flour mixture, beating until blended. Stir in the raisins and coconut by hand. Spoon the batter into the prepared pans.

Bake for 50–60 minutes, until a toothpick inserted into the center comes out clean. Cool the cakes completely in the pans on racks. When cool, run a knife around the cakes to loosen. Invert onto racks and remove the paper. Turn over, rounded side up. Using serrated knife, trim the rounded tops to level.

Cream Cheese Frosting Beat the cream cheese and butter in a bowl until smooth. Beat in the rum and vanilla. Add the confectioners' sugar, beating until just smooth. Place a cake layer on a serving plate. Spread with half of the frosting. Top with the remaining cake layer, trimmed side down. Spread with the remaining frosting. Sprinkle with the extra coconut.

SERVES 12 • PREPARATION 30 MIN. • COOKING 50–60 MIN. • LEVEL 2

19 chocolate cream roulade

- 3 ounces (90 g) dark chocolate, chopped
- 1/2 cup (75 g) all-purpose (plain) flour
- 1/2 teaspoon baking powder
- 1/2 teaspoon baking soda (bicarbonate of soda)
- 1/4 teaspoon salt
- 4 large eggs
- 3/4 cup (150 g) sugar
- 1 teaspoon vanilla extract (essence)
- 2 tablespoons cold water
- Confectioners' (icing) sugar, to dust
- 1 recipe chantilly cream (see page 196)
- 2 cups (300 g) fresh raspberries

Preheat the oven to 375°F (190°C/gas 5). Butter a 10 x 15-inch (25 x 35-cm) jelly-roll pan. Line with parchment paper. Melt the chocolate in a double boiler over barely simmering water. Sift the flour, baking powder, baking soda, and salt into a bowl. Beat the eggs, sugar, and vanilla in a bowl with an electric mixer on medium speed until pale and thick. Fold in the flour mixture, water, and chocolate. Spoon into the pan.

Bake for 15–20 minutes, until springy to the touch. Cool in the pan for 5 minutes. Dust a kitchen towel with confectioners' sugar. Turn the cake out onto the towel and remove the paper. Roll up, using the towel as a guide. Leave, seam-side down, until cool. Unroll the cake and spread with the chantilly. Sprinkle with the raspberries and reroll. Dust with confectioners' sugar.

SERVES 8 • PREPARATION 30 MIN. • COOKING 15–20 MIN. • LEVEL 3

20 coffee cream roulade

- 1 cup (150 g) all-purpose (plain) flour
- 1 teaspoon baking powder
- 5 large eggs
- 1 cup (200 g) sugar
- ⅓ cup (90 g) salted butter, melted
- 2 tablespoons freeze-dried coffee granules dissolved in 1 tablespoon boiling water
- 1 recipe chantilly cream (see page 196), flavored with 2 tablespoons freeze-dried coffee granules
- Confectioners' (icing) sugar, to dust

Preheat the oven to 400°F (200°C/gas 6). Butter a 10 x 15-inch (25 x 35-cm) jelly-roll pan. Line with parchment paper. Sift the flour and baking powder into a bowl. Beat the eggs and sugar in a bowl with an electric mixer on medium speed until pale and thick. With mixer at low speed, beat in the flour mixture, melted butter, and coffee mixture. Spoon the batter into the prepared pan.

Bake for 15–20 minutes, until springy to the touch. Cool in the pan for 5 minutes. Dust a clean kitchen towel with confectioners' sugar. Turn the cake out onto the towel and remove the paper. Roll up the cake, using the towel as a guide. Leave, seam-side down, until cool. Unroll the cake, spread with the coffee-flavored chantilly, and reroll. Dust with confectioners' sugar.

SERVES 8 • PREPARATION 30 MIN. • COOKING 15–20 MIN. • LEVEL 3

1 mexican wedding cakes

2 italian shortbread

3 greek shortbread

4 panforte

5 almond biscotti

6 new zealand ginger crunch

7 portuguese custard tarts

8 australian cupcakes

9 pistachio baklava

10 lebanese almond pastries

11 moroccan almond pastries

12
mexican three milk cake

13
almond & cranberry danish

14
apple & blackberry strudel

global baking

15
sachertorte

16
pumpkin pie

17
breton custard tart

18
black forest cake

19
viennois

20
viennese walnut torte

1 mexican wedding cakes

- 2 cups (300 g) all-purpose (plain) flour
- 1 teaspoon ground cinnamon
- 1 cup (150 g) blanched almonds, lightly toasted
- 1 cup (250 g) salted butter, softened
- 1/2 cup (100 g) superfine (caster) sugar
- 1 cup (150 g) confectioners' (icing) sugar to dust

Preheat the oven to 350°F (180°C/gas 4). Line two baking sheets with parchment paper. Mix the flour and cinnamon in a bowl. Chop the almonds in a food processor to make fine crumbs. Add to the flour mixture. Beat the butter and sugar in a bowl with an electric mixer on medium speed until pale and creamy. With the mixer on low speed, beat in the flour mixture.

Shape the dough into 25 balls. Place on the prepared baking sheets, spacing well. Gently press to flatten slightly. Bake for 20–25 minutes, until golden brown. Cool on the sheets until the cookies firm slightly. Transfer to racks and let cool completely. Dust with the confectioners' sugar just before serving.

MAKES 25 • PREPARATION 15 MIN. • COOKING 20–25 MIN. • LEVEL 1

2 italian shortbread

- $3\frac{1}{3}$ cups (500 g) all-purpose (plain) flour
- 1 teaspoon salt
- $1\frac{2}{3}$ cups (400 g) unsalted butter, softened
- 1 cup (200 g) sugar
- 3 large eggs + 1 large egg white, lightly beaten
- 2 teaspoons vanilla extract (essence)
- 1 cup (150 g) confectioners' (icing) sugar, to dust

Combine the flour and salt in a large bowl. Use your fingertips to rub in the butter until the mixture resembles coarse crumbs. Stir in the sugar. Add the eggs and vanilla. Mix to make a soft dough. Cover the bowl with a clean kitchen towel and let rest for 1 hour.

Preheat the oven to 350°F (180°C/gas 4). Line four baking sheets with parchment paper. Roll out the dough on a floured work surface to ½ inch (1 cm) thick. Cut out the cookies using flower-shaped cookie cutters. Transfer to the baking sheets. Brush with the beaten egg white. Bake for 20 minutes, until golden brown. Let cool on the baking sheets for 2–3 minutes, then transfer to wire racks to cool completely. Dust with the confectioners' sugar just before serving.

MAKES 40–50 • PREPARATION 15 MIN. + 1 HR. TO REST • COOKING 20 MIN. • LEVEL 1

3 greek shortbread

- 1 cup (250 g) salted butter, softened
- $^{3}/_{4}$ cup (150 g) superfine (caster) sugar
- 1 large egg
- $^{1}/_{2}$ teaspoon vanilla extract (essence)
- $^{1}/_{2}$ teaspoon almond extract (essence)
- 2 cups (300 g) all-purpose (plain) flour
- 1 large egg, beaten

Preheat the oven to 400°F (200°C/gas 6). Butter two large baking sheets or line with parchment paper.

Beat the butter and sugar in a medium bowl with an electric mixer on medium speed until pale and creamy. Add the egg and beat until just combined.

With the mixer on low speed, beat in the vanilla and almond extracts, followed by the flour. You will have a fairly firm dough.

Take a spoonful of dough at a time and shape into twists, 'S' shapes, or wreaths. Place the cookies 2 inches (5 cm) apart on the prepared baking sheets. Brush with beaten egg.

Bake for 10–15 minutes, until lightly browned and firm. Let the cookies cool on the baking sheets until they harden a little, 2–3 minutes. Transfer to racks and let cool completely.

MAKES 28–30 • PREPARATION 20 MIN. • COOKING 10–15 MIN. • LEVEL 1

This shortbread is known as koulourakia in Greece. It is traditionally baked at Easter.

4 panforte

- 1 cup (180 g) candied (glacé) orange peel, chopped
- 2 tablespoons candied (glacé) lemon peel, chopped
- $1\frac{2}{3}$ cups (200 g) unblanched, toasted almonds, coarsely chopped
- $\frac{2}{3}$ cup (90 g) walnuts, coarsely chopped
- 1 cup (150 g) all-purpose (plain) flour
- 3 tablespoons ground cardamom
- 1 tablespoon ground cinnamon
- $\frac{1}{2}$ teaspoon each ground coriander, mace, cloves, and nutmeg
- 1 cup (200 g) firmly packed brown sugar
- $\frac{1}{2}$ cup (120 ml) honey
- $\frac{1}{4}$ cup (60 ml) boiling water + extra, as needed
- $\frac{1}{3}$ cup (50 g) confectioners' (icing) sugar, to dust

Preheat the oven to 350°F (180°C/gas 4). Line a baking sheet with rice paper. Mix the candied peels, almonds, walnuts, flour, and spices in a large bowl. Heat the brown sugar, honey, and water in a saucepan over medium heat, stirring until the sugar has dissolved. Cook, without stirring, until small bubbles form on the surface and the syrup reaches the soft-ball stage, 5–10 minutes. Stir into the nut mixture. The mixture should be very firm; add more boiling water if it is too firm.

Pour onto the prepared sheet. Shape into a round about 1 inch (2.5 cm) thick. Bake for 25–35 minutes, until golden brown. Cool on the baking sheet. Dust with confectioners' sugar.

SERVES 12 • PREPARATION 25 MIN. • COOKING 30–45 MIN. • LEVEL 1

5 almond biscotti

- $1\frac{1}{2}$ cups (200 g) whole unblanched almonds
- 2 cups (300 g) all-purpose (plain) flour
- $\frac{1}{2}$ cup (100 g) sugar
- $\frac{1}{2}$ teaspoon baking powder
- $\frac{1}{2}$ teaspoon baking soda (bicarbonate of soda)
- $\frac{1}{4}$ teaspoon salt
- 3 large eggs, lightly beaten
- 1 teaspoon vanilla extract (essence)
- 1 teaspoon finely grated organic lemon zest
- 1 large egg white, lightly beaten

Preheat the oven to 350°F (180°C/gas 4). Line three baking sheets with parchment paper. Spread the almonds on a baking sheet and toast until golden, about 5 minutes. Finely chop one-third of the almonds in a food processor. Chop the remaining nuts coarsely.

Combine the flour, sugar, baking powder, baking soda, and salt in a bowl. Add the eggs, vanilla, and lemon zest. Beat until well combined. Knead for 3 minutes, working in the almonds. Divide the dough in three, and roll each third into a log about 1 inch (2.5 cm) thick. Place on one of the baking sheets. Flatten slightly and brush with egg white. Bake for 20 minutes. Let cool for 5 minutes then cut diagonally into 1-inch (2.5-cm) thick cookies. Place on the baking sheets. Bake for 10–15 minutes, until crisp and golden brown. Cool on racks.

MAKES 25–30 • PREPARATION 40 MIN. • COOKING 35–40 MIN. • LEVEL 2

6 new zealand ginger crunch

Ginger Crunch
- $^{2}/_{3}$ cup (150 g) salted butter, softened
- $^{1}/_{2}$ cup (100 g) sugar
- 2 cups (300 g) all-purpose (plain) flour
- 2 teaspoons ground ginger
- 1 teaspoon baking powder

Ginger Frosting
- 2 cups (300 g) confectioners' (icing) sugar
- 2 tablespoons ground ginger
- $^{1}/_{4}$ cup (60 ml) light corn (golden) syrup
- $^{1}/_{2}$ cup (125 g) salted butter, cubed

Ginger Crunch Preheat the oven to 350°F (180°C/gas 4). Line a rectangular 13 x 9 inch (32 x 23 cm) baking pan with aluminum foil, leaving plenty of foil overhanging the edges.

Beat the butter and sugar in a bowl with an electric mixer on medium speed until pale and creamy. With the mixer on low speed, beat in the flour, ginger, and baking powder until a dough begins to form. Turn out onto a clean work surface and knead to fully combine. Press the dough into the prepared baking pan, smoothing with the back of a spoon to create an even surface. Bake for 15–20 minutes, until golden brown. Set aside on a rack.

Ginger Frosting Combine the confectioners' sugar and ginger in a small saucepan. Add the corn syrup and butter and warm over low heat, stirring occasionally, until the butter and syrup have melted into the confectioners' sugar to form a frosting. Pour over the warm ginger crunch base, tilting the pan slightly to spread evenly. Cover and set aside in a cool place until set, about 4 hours.

Lift out onto a clean chopping board using the overhanging foil. Dip a sharp knife into boiling water and cut the ginger crunch into 24 squares.

MAKES 24 • PREPARATION 20 MIN. + 4 HR. TO SET • COOKING 15–20 MIN. • LEVEL 1

7 portuguese custard tarts

- 2 (8-ounce/250-g) sheets ready-rolled puff pastry
- 1 cup (200 g) sugar
- ⅓ cup (90 ml) water
- 3 tablespoons cornstarch (cornflour)
- 2 cups (500 ml) milk
- 4 large egg yolks, lightly beaten
- 1 teaspoon vanilla extract (essence)

Butter a standard 12-cup muffin pan. Cut twelve pastry rounds, fit into the prepared muffin pans and refrigerate. Heat the sugar and water in a medium saucepan over medium-low heat, stirring until the sugar dissolves. Combine the cornstarch, and ¼ cup (60 ml) of milk in a bowl, stirring until smooth. Add the remaining milk, egg yolks, and vanilla, stirring until combined. Pour the egg mixture into the sugar syrup and cook over low heat, stirring until thickened. Transfer the custard to a medium bowl, cover with parchment paper, and refrigerate until cool.

Preheat the oven to 425°F (220°C/gas 7). Spoon the custard into the pastry bases. Bake for 30 minutes, until custard is set and the tops are pale golden brown. Let cool a little in the pans. Serve warm.

MAKES 12 • PREPARATION 30 MIN. + 1 HR. TO CHILL • COOKING 45 MIN. • LEVEL 2

8 australian cupcakes

Cupcakes
- $1\frac{1}{2}$ cups (225 g) all-purpose (plain) flour
- 2 teaspoons baking powder
- $\frac{1}{2}$ cup (120 g) butter, softened
- $\frac{3}{4}$ cup (150 g) sugar
- 1 teaspoon vanilla extract (essence)
- $\frac{1}{2}$ cup (120 ml) milk
- 2 large eggs, lightly beaten

Raspberry Glaze
- 1 (3-ounce/85-g) packet raspberry jell-o (jelly) crystals
- 1 cup (250 ml) boiling water
- $\frac{1}{2}$ cup (125 g) ice
- $1\frac{1}{2}$ cups (185 g) shredded (desiccated) coconut
- $\frac{1}{2}$ cup (125 ml) whipped cream

Cupcakes Preheat the oven to 325°F (170°C/gas 3). Butter a standard 12-cup muffin pan. Combine the flour and baking powder in a bowl. Beat the butter, sugar, and vanilla in a large bowl with an electric mixer on medium speed until pale and creamy. Add the milk and eggs, beating until just blended. Fold in the flour mixture. Spoon the batter into the prepared cups. Bake for 25–30 minutes, until golden brown. Let cool in the pans for 5 minutes. Turn out onto racks and let cool completely.

Raspberry Glaze Mix the jell-o crystals and water in a medium bowl until the crystals have dissolved. Add the ice and let it melt. Refrigerate for 10 minutes, until the jell-o has set slightly. Dip the cupcakes in the jell-o. Dip in the coconut. Place on racks to set for 15 minutes. Cut each cupcake in half, fill with whipped cream, and sandwich together again.

MAKES 12 • PREPARATION 40 MIN. • COOKING 25–30 MIN. • LEVEL 2

9 pistachio baklava

- $1^3/_4$ cups (350 g) + 8 tablespoons sugar, divided
- $1^1/_4$ cups (300 ml) freshly squeezed orange juice
- $1^1/_2$ teaspoons ground cardamom
- 12 ounces (350 g) shelled pistachios, toasted (scant 3 cups)
- 2 teaspoons ground cinnamon
- 1 cup (250 g) salted butter, melted
- 30 (14 x 9-inch/35 x 23-cm) sheets filo (phyllo) pastry

Stir $1^3/_4$ cups (350 g) of sugar with the orange juice in saucepan over medium heat until the sugar dissolves. Bring to a boil and simmer until reduced to $1^1/_2$ cups, 8–10 minutes. Add the cardamom. Set aside to cool. Combine the pistachios with 2 tablespoons of sugar in a food processor. Process until most of the nuts are finely ground, but leaving some larger pieces. Mix in the remaining 6 tablespoons of sugar and the cinnamon.

Preheat the oven to 350°F (180°C/gas 4). Brush a 13 x 9-inch (33 x 23-cm) baking dish with butter. Place a sheet of filo on the bottom of the dish. Brush lightly with butter. Repeat nine more times with filo and butter. Sprinkle half of the pistachio mixture evenly over the filo. Cover the nuts with a sheet of filo and brush lightly with butter. Repeat nine more times with filo and butter. Sprinkle with the remaining pistachio mixture. Cover with a sheet of filo and brush with butter. Repeat nine more times with filo and butter.

Using a sharp knife, score the top layer of filo from the top left corner to the bottom right corner. Score 1-inch (2.5-cm) parallel rows on both sides of the first cut. Turn the pan and score rows about 2 inches (5 cm) wide, forming a diamond pattern. Bake for 50–55 minutes, until golden brown. Drizzle the hot baklava with the syrup. Cool in the pan on a rack. Cut along the score lines all the way through the layers.

SERVES 16 • PREPARATION 30 MIN. • COOKING 50–55 MIN. • LEVEL 2

10 lebanese almond pastries

Pastry
- 1 pound (500 g) fine semolina
- 1 cup (250 g) butter, melted
- $\frac{1}{2}$ cup (120 ml) rosewater
- $\frac{1}{2}$ cup (120 ml) orange blossom water

Filling
- $\frac{2}{3}$ cup (50 g) ground almonds
- $\frac{1}{3}$ cup (30 g) shelled walnuts, crushed
- $\frac{1}{3}$ cup (30 g) shelled pistachio, crushed
- $\frac{1}{2}$ cup (100 g) sugar
- 1 tablespoon orange blossom water
- Confectioners' (icing) sugar, to dust

Pastry Place the semolina in a large bowl and stir in the butter. Cover and let rest overnight at room temperature. Next day, stir in the rosewater and orange blossom water and mix into a dough. Preheat the oven to 350°F (180°C/gas 4). Lightly oil two baking sheets.

Filling Combine all the filling ingredients in a bowl and mix well. Take heaped teaspoons of dough, shape into balls, and make hollows in the centers with your finger. Stuff a little of the filling into each hollow and seal the opening. Place on the baking sheets. Bake for 10–15 minutes, until golden brown. Let cool on racks until firm. Dust with confectioners' sugar before serving.

SERVES 10–12 • PREPARATION 1 HR. + 12 HR. TO REST • COOKING 15 MIN. • LEVEL 2

11 moroccan almond pastries

Syrup
- $1\frac{1}{2}$ cups (300 g) sugar
- $1\frac{1}{2}$ cups (370 ml) water
- 3 cinnamon sticks, broken in half
- Seeds from 1 vanilla bean

Filling
- $1\frac{1}{2}$ cups (250 g) whole almonds, toasted
- 1 teaspoon ground cinnamon
- 3 large eggs
- $1\frac{1}{2}$ cups (225 g) confectioners' (icing) sugar
- $\frac{1}{4}$ teaspoon baking powder
- 12 sheets filo (phyllo) pastry
- $\frac{3}{4}$ cup (180 g) salted butter, melted

Syrup Stir all the ingredients in a pan over medium heat until the sugar dissolves. Simmer for 5 minutes.

Filling Finely chop the almonds and cinnamon in a food processor. Beat the eggs, confectioners' sugar, and baking powder in a bowl until thick. Beat in the almond mixture. Chill until thick, at least 3 hours. Preheat the oven to 375°F (190°C/gas 5). Oil a baking sheet. Place a sheet of filo on a work surface. Brush with butter. Cut lengthwise into three $3\frac{1}{2}$-inch (9-cm) wide strips. Place a tablespoon of filling at a short end of one strip. Fold a corner of filo over the filling. Repeat the folding down the length of the strip to form a triangle. Brush with butter. Place on the baking sheet. Repeat with the remaining pastry, butter, and filling. Bake for 15–20 minutes, until golden. Drizzle with syrup and let cool.

MAKES 30–36 • PREPARATION 45 MIN. + 3 HR TO COOL • COOKING 15–20 MIN. • LEVEL 2

12 mexican three milk cake

Cake
- 1½ cups (180 g) all-purpose (plain) flour
- 1½ teaspoons baking powder
- Pinch of salt
- 5 large eggs, separated
- 1 cup (200 g) superfine (caster) sugar
- 1 teaspoon vanilla extract (essence)
- ¼ cup (60 ml) milk
- Confectioners' (icing) sugar, to dust

Milk Syrup
- 1 (14-ounce/400-ml) can sweetened condensed milk
- 1½ cups (375 ml) canned evaporated milk
- ¾ cup (180 ml) light (single) cream
- 1 tablespoon dark rum
- 1 teaspoon vanilla extract (essence)

Cake Preheat the oven to 350°F (180°C/gas 4). Line a 10-inch (25-cm) springform pan with parchment paper. Sift the flour, baking powder, and salt into a small bowl. Beat the egg yolks, ¾ cup (150 g) of sugar, and vanilla in a bowl with an electric mixer on medium speed until pale and thick. With the mixer on low speed, add the flour mixture and milk alternately, beating until just combined. Beat the egg whites in a medium bowl until soft peaks begin to form. Gradually add the remaining ¼ cup (50 g) sugar, beating until thick and glossy. Fold a large spoonful of the whites into the yolk mixture. Fold in the remaining whites. Pour the mixture into the prepared pan. Bake for 35–40 minutes, until springy to the touch and a toothpick inserted into the center comes out clean. Let cool in the pan for 15 minutes.

Milk Syrup Place all the syrup ingredients in a medium bowl and whisk to combine. Poke holes in the cake with a skewer. Slowly pour the syrup over the cake, waiting for each addition to be absorbed before adding the next. Dust the cake with confectioners' sugar and serve.

SERVES 12 • PREPARATION 25 MIN. + 15 MIN. TO COOL • COOKING 35–40 MIN. • LEVEL 2

This cake comes from Mexico and Central America and is known in Spanish as Pastel de tres leche.

13 almond & cranberry danish

- 1 (8-ounce/250-g) sheet ready-rolled puff pastry
- 3 tablespoons butter
- 1/4 cup (50 g) sugar
- 2 large eggs
- 1/3 cup (50 g) finely ground almonds
- 3 tablespoons dried cranberries
- 2 tablespoons all-purpose (plain) flour + extra to dust
- 1/2 teaspoon vanilla extract (essence)
- 5 tablespoons apricot preserves (jam)
- 1/2 cup (75 g) confectioners' (icing) sugar
- 2 teaspoons boiling water

Preheat the oven to 400°F (200°C/gas 6). Oil a baking sheet. Cut the pastry sheet in half lengthwise. Beat the butter and sugar until pale and creamy. Beat in one egg, the almonds, cranberries, flour, and vanilla. Spoon half the filling down one long edge of each large piece of pastry. Spoon the apricot preserves alongside the filling. Beat the remaining egg and brush the edges of the pastry. Roll up lengthwise, pinching the ends to seal. Transfer to the baking sheet. Brush with beaten egg. Cover and chill overnight.

Preheat the oven to 400°F (200°C/gas 6). Bake for 20–25 minutes, until golden brown. Mix the confectioner's sugar with the water. Drizzle over the warm Danish and serve.

SERVES 6 • PREPARATION 30 MIN. + 12 HR. TO CHILL • COOKING 20–25 MIN. • LEVEL 2

14 apple & blackberry strudel

- 2 Granny Smith apples, peeled, cored, and thinly sliced
- $\frac{1}{2}$ cup (120 g) + 2 tablespoons salted butter, melted
- $1\frac{1}{2}$ cups (200 g) blackberries
- $\frac{3}{4}$ cup (150 g) sugar
- $\frac{1}{2}$ cup (90 g) dried apricots, finely chopped
- 1 cup (150 g) pecans, toasted and coarsely chopped
- 1 teaspoon ground cinnamon
- 6 sheets filo (phyllo) pastry, thawed if frozen
- $\frac{1}{4}$ cup (30 g) fine dry bread crumbs

Preheat the oven to 425°F (220°C/gas 7). Oil a large baking sheet. Sauté the apples in 2 tablespoons of butter in a large frying pan over medium heat for 5 minutes. Stir in the blackberries and sugar and simmer for 10 minutes. Stir in the apricots, pecans, and cinnamon. Drain any juice and set aside to cool. Brush a first sheet of filo with melted butter. Sprinkle with some bread crumbs. Top with another sheet of filo and brush with butter. Repeat with 4 more sheets, finishing with a filo layer. Spread the blackberry mixture over the pastry and carefully roll it up. Transfer to the baking sheet and place seam-side down. Brush with the remaining butter. Bake for 20–25 minutes, until lightly browned. Serve warm or at room temperature.

SERVES 6 • PREPARATION 20 MIN. • COOKING 20–25 MIN. • LEVEL 2

15 sachertorte

Cake
- 5 ounces (150 g) dark chocolate, coarsely chopped
- 1/3 cup (90 g) salted butter, softened
- 1/2 cup (100 g) sugar
- 5 large eggs, separated
- 2/3 cup (100 g) all-purpose (plain) flour
- 1/3 cup (100 g) apricot preserves (jam)

Frosting
- 1 tablespoon salted butter
- 4 ounces (120 g) dark chocolate, coarsely chopped
- 1/3 cup (90 ml) strong black coffee, cold
- 2 cups (300 g) confectioners' (icing) sugar
- 2 teaspoons vanilla extract (essence)

Cake Preheat the oven to 325°F (160°C/gas 3). Set out a 9-inch (23-cm) springform pan. Melt the chocolate in a double boiler over barely simmering water. Beat the butter and sugar in a bowl with an electric mixer at medium speed until pale and creamy. Add the egg yolks one at a time, beating until just blended after each addition. Fold in the chocolate and flour. With the mixer on high speed, beat the egg whites until stiff. Fold into the batter. Spoon into the prepared pan.

Bake for 55–60 minutes, until a toothpick inserted into the center comes out clean. Cool the cake in the pan for 20 minutes. Loosen and remove the pan sides and let cool completely. Split the cake horizontally. Place one layer on a serving plate. Spread with the apricot preserves. Top with the remaining cake.

Frosting Melt the butter and chocolate in a double boiler. Add the coffee, confectioners' sugar and vanilla. Beat until smooth and creamy. Spread the top and sides of the cake with the frosting. Let set before serving.

SERVES 8–10 • PREPARATION 30 MIN. • COOKING 55–60 MIN. • LEVEL 2

This classic Austrian cake was invented by Franz Sacher in Vienna in 1832. Sacher was an apprentice chef in the house of Prince Metternich at the time, and the request to create a special dessert for important guests fell on him because the head chef was ill.

16 pumpkin pie

Crust
- $1\frac{1}{2}$ recipes shortcrust pastry (see page 106)

Pumpkin Filling
- $1\frac{3}{4}$ cups (400 g) canned or fresh pumpkin purée
- 3 large eggs, lightly beaten
- $\frac{1}{2}$ cup (100 g) firmly packed light brown sugar
- 1 cup (250 ml) heavy (double) cream
- 1 tablespoon all-purpose (plain) flour
- 1 teaspoon ground cinnamon
- $\frac{1}{4}$ teaspoon ground ginger
- $\frac{1}{4}$ teaspoon ground nutmeg
- $\frac{1}{8}$ teaspoon ground cloves
- Whipped cream or crème fraîche, to serve

Crust Prepare the pastry. Divide into two portions, one twice as large as the other. Wrap in plastic wrap (cling film) and refrigerate for 1 hour. Roll out the larger piece of pastry on a floured work surface to $\frac{1}{8}$ inch (3 mm) thick. Line a 9-inch (23-cm) pie pan with the pastry. Chill both pieces of pastry for 30 minutes.

Pumpkin Filling Preheat the oven to 350°F (180°C/gas 4). Combine all the filling ingredients—except the whipped cream—in a bowl, stirring to combine. Pour into the prepared pie crust. Roll out the remaining piece of pastry and place on top, pressing down on the edges to seal. Make a few small slits in the top with a knife to let steam escape during baking. Bake for 45–55 minutes, until golden brown. Serve warm with a dollop of whipped cream or crème fraîche.

SERVES 8–10 • PREPARATION 30 MIN. + $1\frac{1}{2}$ HR. TO CHILL
COOKING 45–55 MIN. • LEVEL 2

17 breton custard tart

- 2 cups (500 ml) milk
- 3 large eggs
- $^1/_2$ cup (100 g) sugar
- 5 tablespoons (75 g) salted butter, melted and cooled
- $^1/_4$ teaspoon vanilla extract (essence)
- $^3/_4$ cup (120 g) all-purpose (plain) flour
- 1 cup (180 g) small pitted prunes
- $^1/_2$ cup (120 ml) water
- $^1/_3$ cup (40 g) raisins
- $^1/_4$ cup (60 ml) Armagnac or other brandy
- Confectioners' (icing) sugar, to dust

Whisk the milk, eggs, sugar, butter, and vanilla until smooth. Add the flour and beat until just blended. Cover and chill for 3 hours.

Heat the prunes, water, and raisins in a small pan over medium heat until softened, about 10 minutes. Turn off the heat. Pour in the brandy. Using a long match, ignite the brandy. Let the flames burn off, shaking the pan occasionally. Transfer the prunes to a bowl and let cool.

Preheat the oven to 375°F (190°C/gas 5). Butter an 8-inch (20-cm) cake pan. Pour the batter into the pan. Spoon the prune mixture over the top. Bake for 1 hour, until puffed and golden. Cool in the pan on a rack. Dust with confectioners' sugar just before serving.

SERVES 8–12 • PREPARATION 30 MIN. + 3 HR. TO CHILL • COOKING $1^1/_4$ HR. • LEVEL 2

18 black forest cake

Chocolate Cake
- $1\frac{1}{3}$ cups (200 g) all-purpose (plain) flour
- 4 tablespoons unsweetened cocoa powder
- 4 ounces (120 g) dark chocolate, coarsely chopped
- 6 large eggs, separated
- 1 cup (200 g) firmly packed light brown sugar
- $\frac{3}{4}$ cup (180 g) salted butter, melted and cooled

Vanilla Cream
- $3\frac{1}{2}$ cups (875 ml) heavy (double) cream
- 7 tablespoons confectioners' (icing) sugar
- 2 teaspoons vanilla extract (essence)

To Decorate
- $\frac{1}{4}$ cup (60 ml) cherry liqueur
- 2 cups (500 ml) maraschino cherries, pitted
- 3 ounces (90 g) dark chocolate, grated
- Dark chocolate curls

Chocolate Cake Preheat the oven to 350°F (180°C/gas 4). Butter a 9-inch (23-cm) round cake pan and line with parchment paper. Mix the flour and cocoa in a bowl. Melt the chocolate in a double boiler over barely simmering water. Beat the egg yolks and brown sugar in a bowl with an electric mixer on medium until creamy. Stir in the chocolate. Beat the egg whites in a bowl with an electric mixer on medium speed until firm peaks form. Fold the egg whites, flour mixture, and butter into the batter.

Spoon the batter into the prepared cake pan. Bake for 45 minutes, until golden brown and a toothpick inserted into the center comes out clean. Let cool in the pan for 10 minutes then turn out onto a rack. Peel off the paper and let cool completely.

Vanilla Cream Beat the cream, sugar, and vanilla in a bowl until thick. Slice the cake into thirds horizontally and brush each layer with cherry liqueur. Spread a layer of cake with a quarter of the vanilla cream and a quarter of the cherries. Cover with a cake layer and spread with cherries and cream. Cover with the remaining cake layer and spread the top and sides with the remaining vanilla cream. Top with the remaining cherries. Coat the sides of the cake with grated chocolate. Decorate the top with the chocolate curls.

SERVES 8–12 • PREPARATION 45 MIN. • COOKING 45 MIN. • LEVEL 3

19 viennois

- $\frac{1}{4}$ cup (30 g) unsweetened cocoa powder
- 3 tablespoons cake flour
- 2 tablespoons cornstarch (cornflour)
- $\frac{1}{4}$ teaspoon salt
- $1\frac{1}{2}$ cups (300 g) sugar
- 8 large eggs, separated
- 2 ounces (60 g) dark chocolate curls
- 2 recipes chocolate ganache (see page 130)

Preheat the oven to 300°F (150°C/gas 2). Line two 8-inch (20-cm) round cake pans with parchment paper. Mix the cocoa, flour, cornstarch, and salt in a bowl. Beat the sugar and egg yolks until pale and thick. With mixer on low, gradually beat in the flour mixture. Beat the egg whites until stiff peaks form. Fold into the batter. Spoon the batter into the pans. Bake for 20–25 minutes, until a toothpick inserted into the center comes out clean. Cool in the pans for 10 minutes. Turn out onto racks. Carefully remove the paper and let cool completely.

Split the cakes horizontally. Place one layer on a serving plate and spread with ganache. Repeat with two more layers. Top with the remaining layer. Spread the top and sides with the remaining ganache. Top with the curls.

SERVES 8–12 • PREPARATION 20 MIN. • COOKING 20–25 MIN. • LEVEL 2

20 viennese walnut torte

Torte

- 2 cups (250 g) finely ground walnuts
- 1/3 cup (50 g) all-purpose (plain) flour
- 1/2 teaspoon baking powder
- 1 cup (250 g) salted butter
- 1 1/4 cups (250 g) sugar
- 1 teaspoon vanilla extract (essence)
- 5 large eggs, separated

Chocolate Glaze

- 5 ounces (150 g) dark chocolate, coarsely chopped
- 1/2 cup (125 g) salted butter, softened
- 2/3 cup (150 g) orange marmalade, warmed

Torte Preheat the oven to 350°F (180°C/gas 4). Butter a 9-inch (23-cm) springform pan. Stir the walnuts, flour, and baking powder in a bowl. Beat the butter, half the sugar, and vanilla in a bowl with an electric mixer on medium speed until creamy. Beat in the egg yolks one at a time. Beat the egg whites until frothy then beat in the remaining sugar until stiff and glossy. Fold into the batter. Fold in the walnut mixture. Spoon into the pan. Bake for 50–60 minutes, until a toothpick inserted into the center comes out clean. Cool in the pan for 10 minutes. Invert onto a rack and let cool completely.

Chocolate Glaze Melt the chocolate in a double boiler. Remove from the heat and stir in the butter. Split the cake in half. Spread one layer with the marmalade. Top with the remaining layer. Drizzle with the glaze.

SERVES 8–12 • PREPARATION 30 MIN. • COOKING 50–60 MIN. • LEVEL 2

1
yo yos

2
monte carlos

3
afghan cookies

4
lemon cheesecake squares

5
marbled cheesecake squares

6
chocolate chip wedges

7
vanilla cupcakes with honey & figs

8
rosewater cupcakes with pistachios

9
party cupcakes

10
cherry tart

11
apricot & almond tart

12
passionfruit tart

13
peach pie

14
berryfruit pie

editor's choice

15
lemon upside-down polenta cake

16
chocolate banana cake

17
peanut butter cake

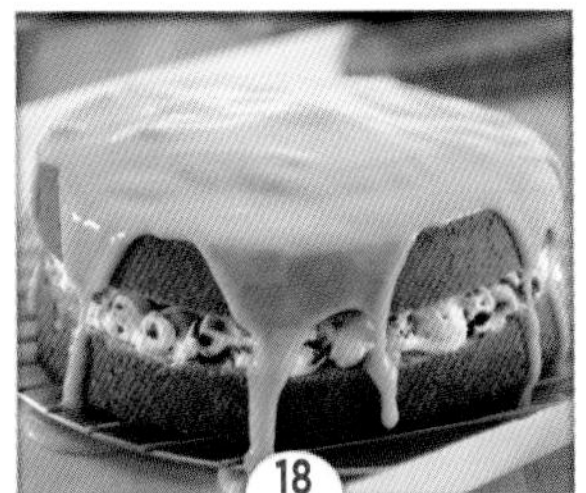
18
blueberry cream cake with cinnamon frosting

19
coffee cream dacquoise

20
orange meringue torte

1 yo yos

Cookies

- 3/4 cup (180 g) salted butter, softened
- 1/3 cup (50 g) confectioners' (icing) sugar
- 1/2 teaspoon vanilla extract (essence)
- 1 1/2 cups (225 g) all-purpose (plain) flour
- 1 teaspoon baking powder
- 1/3 cup (50 g) custard powder

Vanilla Butter Filling

- 1/4 cup (60 g) salted butter, softened
- 1/2 cup (75 g) confectioners' (icing) sugar
- 1/2 teaspoon vanilla extract (essence)
- 2 tablespoons custard powder

Cookies Preheat the oven to 350°F (180°C/gas 4). Line two baking sheets with parchment paper. Beat the butter, confectioners' sugar, and vanilla with an electric mixer on medium speed until pale and creamy. Combine the flour, baking powder, and custard powder in a bowl. With the mixer on low speed, gradually beat in the flour mixture. Roll into 30 small balls and place on the prepared baking sheets, spacing well. Flatten slightly with a fork. Bake for 15–20 minutes, until pale golden brown. Let cool on the baking sheets for 2–3 minutes. Transfer to a rack and let cool completely.

Vanilla Butter Filling Beat all the filling ingredients until pale and creamy. Spread half of the cooled cookies with the filling. Place the remaining cookies on top and gently sandwich together.

MAKES 15 • PREPARATION 20 MIN. • COOKING 15–20 MIN. • LEVEL 1

2 monte carlos

Cookies
- $1\frac{1}{2}$ cups (225 g) all-purpose (plain) flour
- 1 teaspoon baking powder
- $\frac{1}{4}$ cup (30 g) custard powder
- $\frac{1}{3}$ cup (50 g) shredded (desiccated) coconut
- $\frac{1}{2}$ cup (120 g) salted butter, softened
- $\frac{1}{2}$ cup (100 g) superfine (caster) sugar
- $\frac{1}{4}$ cup (60 ml) milk

Coconut Butter Filling
- $\frac{1}{3}$ cup (90 g) salted butter, softened
- $\frac{2}{3}$ cup (100 g) confectioners' (icing) sugar
- 3 teaspoons milk
- 2 tablespoons shredded (desiccated) coconut
- $\frac{1}{2}$ cup (150 g) raspberry preserves (jam)

Cookies Preheat the oven to 350°F (180°C/gas 4). Line three baking sheets with parchment paper. Combine the flour, baking powder, custard powder, and coconut in a medium bowl. Beat the butter and sugar with an electric mixer on medium speed until pale and creamy. With the mixer on low speed, gradually beat in the flour mixture and milk. Roll forty small balls and place on the baking sheets, spacing well. Flatten slightly with a fork. Bake for 15–20 minutes, until firm and pale golden brown. Let cool on the baking sheets for 2–3 minutes. Transfer to a rack and let cool completely.

Coconut Butter Filling Beat the butter and confectioners' sugar until pale and creamy. Stir in the milk and coconut. Spread half of the cooled cookies with the filling. Spread the remaining cookies with raspberry preserves. Sandwich the two halves together.

MAKES 20 • PREPARATION 30 MIN. • COOKING 15–20 MIN. • LEVEL 1

3 afghan cookies

Cookies
- $^3/_4$ cup (180 g) salted butter, softened
- $^1/_2$ cup (100 g) sugar
- $1^1/_3$ cups (175 g) all-purpose (plain) flour
- $^1/_4$ cup (30 g) unsweetened cocoa powder
- 2 cups (200 g) cornflakes
- $^1/_3$ cup (40 g) shredded (desiccated) coconut
- $^1/_4$ cup (30 g) walnuts, coarsely chopped

Chocolate Frosting
- 1 cup (150 g) confectioners' (icing) sugar
- 2 tablespoons unsweetened cocoa powder
- $^1/_2$ teaspoon vanilla extract (essence)
- 2 tablespoons boiling water

Cookies Preheat the oven to 350°F (180°C/gas 4). Line two large baking sheets with parchment paper. Beat the butter and sugar with an electric mixer on medium speed until pale and creamy. With the mixer on low speed, gradually add the flour and cocoa, beating until combined. Stir in the cornflakes and coconut by hand. Spoon 25 mounds of mixture onto the prepared cookie sheets, spacing about 1 inch (2.5 cm) apart.

Bake for 15–20 minutes, until firm to the touch. Let cool on the baking sheets for 2–3 minutes. Transfer to a rack and let cool completely.

Chocolate Frosting Combine the confectioners' sugar and cocoa in a small bowl. Add the vanilla and gradually pour in enough of the water to obtain a spreadable frosting. Frost the tops of the cooled cookies and top with chopped walnuts.

MAKES 25 • PREPARATION 20 MIN. • COOKING 15–20 MIN. • LEVEL 1

These cookies are known as Afghan biscuits in their homeland of New Zealand. No one knows the origin of the name, but these chewy chocolate and cornflake cookies are a firm favorite Downunder.

4 lemon cheesecake squares

Cookie Base

- $1\frac{1}{4}$ cups (160 g) graham cracker or digestive biscuit crumbs
- $\frac{1}{3}$ cup (90 g) salted butter, melted

Topping

- 8 ounces (250 g) cream cheese, softened
- $\frac{1}{2}$ cup (100 g) sugar
- 5 tablespoons lemon curd
- 3 tablespoons cornstarch (cornflour)
- 1 large egg, lightly beaten

Cookie Base Preheat the oven to 375°F (190°C/gas 5). Butter a 9-inch (23-cm) square baking pan. Mix the graham cracker crumbs and butter in a large bowl until well blended. Firmly press the mixture into the prepared pan to form a smooth, even layer.

Topping Beat the cream cheese and sugar in a large bowl with an electric mixer on low speed until smooth. Beat in the lemon curd, cornstarch, and egg. Spoon the topping over the cookie base. Bake for 25–30 minutes, until firm to the touch. Let cool completely before cutting into squares.

MAKES 16 • PREPARATION 20 MIN. • COOKING 25–30 MIN. • LEVEL 1

5 marbled cheesecake squares

Cream Cheese Mixture
- 1 cup (250 g) cream cheese, softened
- $^1/_4$ cup (50 g) sugar
- 2 tablespoons finely grated untreated orange zest
- 3 tablespoons freshly squeezed orange juice
- 1 teaspoon cornstarch (cornflour)
- 1 large egg

Chocolate Mixture
- 8 ounces (250 g) dark chocolate, chopped
- $^1/_4$ cup (60 g) salted butter
- $^3/_4$ cup (150 g) sugar
- 2 teaspoons vanilla extract
- 2 large eggs, beaten with 2 tablespoons cold water
- $^1/_2$ cup (75 g) all-purpose (plain) flour

Cream Cheese Mixture Preheat the oven to 350°F (180°C/gas 4). Butter a 9-inch (23-cm) square baking pan. Beat the cream cheese and sugar in a bowl with an electric mixer on high speed until creamy. Beat in the orange zest and juice, cornstarch, and egg.

Chocolate Mixture Melt the chocolate and butter in a double boiler over barely simmering water. Set aside to cool. Stir in the sugar and vanilla. Stir in the beaten egg mixture, followed by the flour.

Pour the chocolate mixture into the pan. Drop spoonfuls of cream cheese mixture on top. Use a knife to swirl the mixtures to create a marbled effect. Bake for 25–30 minutes, until risen around the edges and set in the center. Let cool in the pan before cutting into squares.

MAKES 16 • PREPARATION 30 MIN. • COOKING 25–35 MIN. • LEVEL 2

6 chocolate chip wedges

- $2\frac{1}{4}$ cups (330 g) all-purpose (plain) flour
- 1 teaspoon baking soda (bicarbonate of soda)
- $\frac{1}{2}$ teaspoon salt
- 1 cup (250 g) salted butter, softened
- $\frac{3}{4}$ cup (150 g) sugar
- $\frac{3}{4}$ cup (150 g) firmly packed light brown sugar
- $\frac{1}{2}$ teaspoon vanilla extract (essence)
- 2 large eggs, lightly beaten
- 1 cup (180 g) dark chocolate chips

Preheat the oven to 375°F (190°C/gas 5). Set out a 14-inch (35-cm) pizza pan. Combine the flour, baking soda, and salt in a medium bowl. Beat the butter and both sugars in a large bowl with an electric mixer on medium speed until creamy. Add the vanilla and eggs, beating until just blended. With the mixer on low speed, beat in the flour mixture and chocolate chips. Spread the mixture in the prepared pan.

Bake for 20–25 minutes, until lightly browned. Let cool completely in the pan. Cut into 20 wedges.

MAKES 20 • PREPARATION 15 MIN. • COOKING 20–25 MIN. • LEVEL 1

These simple cookies are popular with all ages but they are especially suited to children who are learning to bake.

7 vanilla cupcakes
with honey & figs

Cupcakes
- 1 cup (150 g) all-purpose (plain) flour
- 1 teaspoon baking powder
- 1/2 cup (100 g) sugar
- 1/4 cup (125 g) salted butter, softened
- 1/4 cup (60 ml) clear honey
- 2 large eggs
- 1 teaspoon vanilla extract (essence)
- 1/2 teaspoon finely grated organic orange zest
- 1/2 cup (90 g) finely chopped dried figs
- 1/4 cup (30 g) finely chopped walnuts

Honey Frosting
- 1/3 cup (90 g) salted butter, softened
- 3 tablespoons (45 ml) clear honey
- 1/2 teaspoon vanilla extract (essence)
- 1 cup (150 g) confectioners' (icing) sugar
- 6 fresh figs, cut into quarters

Cupcakes Preheat the oven to 325°F (170°C/gas 3). Line a standard 12-cup muffin tin with paper liners. Mix the flour, baking powder, and sugar in a bowl. Beat the butter, honey, eggs, vanilla, and orange zest in a bowl until just blended. Beat in the flour mixture, dried figs, and walnuts. Spoon into the cups. Bake for 20–25 minutes, until golden brown. Let cool on wire racks.

Honey Frosting Beat the butter, 1 tablespoon honey, and vanilla seeds in a small bowl. Stir in the confectioners' sugar until well blended. Spread the frosting on the cupcakes. Decorate each cupcake with two fig quarters and drizzle with the remaining honey.

MAKES 12 • PREPARATION 30 MIN. • COOKING 20–25 MIN. • LEVEL 1

8 rosewater cupcakes
with pistachios

Cupcakes
- 3 ounces (90 g) white chocolate, coarsely chopped
- ⅓ cup (90 ml) light (single) cream
- 1 cup (150 g) all-purpose (plain) flour
- ½ cup (50 g) ground pistachios
- 1 teaspoon baking powder
- ⅓ cup (90 g) salted butter, softened
- 1 cup (200 g) sugar
- 2 large eggs
- 2 tablespoons rose water
- 12 pink sugared roses, to decorate

Rose Frosting
- ½ cup (125 g) unsalted butter, softened
- ½ tablespoon rose water
- 1½ cups (225 g) confectioners' (icing) sugar

Cupcakes Preheat the oven to 325°F (170°C/gas 3). Line a standard 12-cup muffin tin with paper liners. Melt the chocolate and cream in a double boiler over barely simmering water. Combine the flour, pistachios, and baking powder. Beat the butter, sugar, and vanilla until creamy. Beat in the eggs. Stir in the flour mixture, chocolate, and rose water. Spoon into the muffin cups. Bake for 20–25 minutes, until golden brown. Let cool.

Rose Frosting Beat the butter, rose water, and confectioners' sugar in a bowl. Transfer to a pastry bag fitted with a star nozzle. Pipe a large rosette of frosting on each cupcake and top with a sugared rose.

MAKES 12 • PREPARATION 30 MIN. • COOKING 20–25 MIN. • LEVEL 1

9 party cupcakes

Cupcakes
- $\frac{3}{4}$ cup (125 g) all-purpose (plain) flour
- 3 tablespoons unsweetened cocoa powder, sifted
- 1 teaspoon baking powder
- $\frac{1}{2}$ cup (125 g) salted butter, softened
- $\frac{3}{4}$ cup (150 g) firmly packed dark brown sugar
- $\frac{1}{2}$ teaspoon vanilla extract (essence)
- 2 large eggs
- 3 tablespoons milk
- $3\frac{1}{2}$ ounces (100 g) mini marshmallows, chopped

Chocolate Buttercream
- 3 ounces (90 g) dark chocolate
- $\frac{1}{2}$ cup (125 g) salted butter, softened
- $\frac{1}{2}$ teaspoon vanilla extract (essence)
- $\frac{1}{2}$ tablespoon milk
- 1 cup (150 g) confectioners' (icing) sugar

To Decorate
- Mini candy-coated chocolate buttons, to decorate
- Colored confectionery sprinkles, to decorate
- 12 small colored candles

Cupcakes Preheat the oven to 350°F (180°C/gas 4). Line a standard 12-cup muffin tin with paper liners. Combine the flour, cocoa, and baking powder in a bowl. Beat the butter, brown sugar, and vanilla in a medium bowl with an electric mixer on medium speed until creamy. Add the eggs one at a time, beating until just blended after each addition. With the mixer on low speed, add the flour mixture, alternating with the milk. Stir the marshmallows in by hand.

Spoon the batter into the prepared cups. Bake for 20–25 minutes, until golden brown and firm to the touch. Transfer the muffin tin to a wire rack. Let cool completely before removing.

Chocolate Buttercream Melt the chocolate in a double boiler over barely simmering water. Let cool. Beat the butter and vanilla in a medium bowl with an electric mixer on medium speed until pale and creamy. Add the milk and chocolate, beating until blended. Gradually add the confectioners' sugar, beating until blended. Spread the buttercream on the cupcakes.

To Decorate Place candy-coated buttons around the outside edge of each cupcake. Sprinkle confectionery sprinkles inside the border and arrange the cupcakes on a plate or cake board. Place a candle in the center of each cupcake and light when ready to serve.

MAKES 12 • PREPARATION 30 MIN. • COOKING 20–25 MIN. • LEVEL 2

10 cherry tart

Crust
- 1 recipe shortcrust pastry (see page 106)

Filling
- 1 cup (250 ml) sour cream
- 3 ounces (90 g) cream cheese, softened
- 1 teaspoon finely grated untreated lemon zest
- 2 large egg yolks
- 1/3 cup (70 g) firmly packed light brown sugar
- 1/2 teaspoon ground cinnamon
- 1 tablespoon cherry liqueur
- 1 pound (500 g) sour cherries, pitted

Crust Prepare the pastry and pre-bake the crust following the instructions on page 106.

Filling Preheat the oven to 350°F (180°C/gas 4). Beat the sour cream, cream cheese, lemon zest, egg yolks, brown sugar, cinnamon, and liqueur in a medium bowl until smooth. Pour the sour cream mixture into the tart crust and arrange the cherries on top. Bake for 35–40 minutes, until golden brown and set. Let cool to room temperature in the pan.

SERVES 6–8 • PREPARATION 30 MIN. + TIME FOR THE CRUST • COOKING 35–40 MIN. • LEVEL 2

11 apricot & almond tart

Crust
- 1 recipe shortcrust pastry (see page 106)

Filling
- $^1/_2$ cup (100 g) superfine (caster) sugar
- $^1/_3$ cup (90 g) salted butter, softened
- $^1/_3$ cup (50 g) all-purpose (plain) flour
- $1^1/_2$ cups (150 g) ground almonds
- 2 large eggs, beaten
- 1 teaspoon vanilla extract (essence)
- 6 ripe apricots, halved and pitted

Crust Prepare the pastry and pre-bake the crust following the instructions on page 106.

Filling Preheat the oven to 325°F (170°C/gas 3). Process the sugar, butter, flour, ground almonds, eggs, and vanilla extract in a food processor on medium speed for 2 minutes, or until a smooth, paste-like mixture is formed. Spoon the almond mixture into the tart crust and smooth with the back of a spoon.

Arrange the apricot halves cut-side down on the tart. Bake for 35–40 minutes, until golden brown. Let cool to room temperature in the pan.

SERVES 6–8 • PREPARATION 30 MIN. + TIME FOR THE CRUST • COOKING 35–40 MIN. • LEVEL 2

12 passionfruit tart

Crust
- 1 recipe shortcrust pastry (see page 106)

Filling
- $1^{3}/_{4}$ cups (350 g) superfine (caster) sugar
- $1^{1}/_{4}$ cups (300 ml) passion fruit pulp, strained
- 1 tablespoon freshly squeezed orange juice
- 1 teaspoon finely grated untreated orange zest
- 7 large egg yolks
- $1^{1}/_{4}$ cups (300 g) salted butter, cubed

Crust Prepare the pastry and pre-bake the crust following the instructions on page 106. Leave to cool while you prepare the filling.

Filling Heat the sugar, passion fruit pulp, and orange juice and zest in a small saucepan over medium heat, stirring until the sugar has dissolved. Beat the egg yolks in a double boiler and gradually pour in the hot passion fruit mixture. Strain through a fine-mesh sieve. Return to the double boiler and place over barely simmering water. Cook, stirring continuously, until the mixture thickens and coats the back of a wooden spoon. Do not allow it to boil.

Remove from the heat and add the butter cubes, one at a time, whisking until fully incorporated. Pour the passion fruit curd into the baked tart crust and smooth using a spatula or the back of a spoon. Refrigerate the tart for 4 hours, until cooled and set.

SERVES 6–8 • PREPARATION 30 MIN. + TIME FOR THE CRUST & 4 HR. TO CHILL • LEVEL 2

The exotic flavors of the passionfruit make this an exquisite tart. Prepare it for dessert to be served at the end of an elegant dinner party. Your guests will love it.

13 peach pie

Crust
- $1\frac{1}{2}$ recipes shortcrust pastry (see page 106)

Filling
- $\frac{1}{3}$ cup (70 g) sugar
- 2 tablespoons all-purpose (plain) flour
- 2 tablespoons ground almonds
- 1 teaspoon ground cinnamon
- 2 pounds (1 kg) peaches, peeled, pitted, and sliced
- 1 tablespoon freshly squeezed lemon juice
- 1 tablespoon salted butter
- 1 large egg, lightly beaten
- 1 tablespoons raw sugar, to sprinkle

Crust Prepare the shortcrust pastry. Divide into two pieces, one slightly larger than the other. Wrap in plastic wrap (cling film) and refrigerate for 1 hour. Roll out the larger piece of pastry on a floured work surface to $\frac{1}{8}$ inch (3 mm) thick. Line the base and sides of a 9-inch (23-cm) pie pan with the pastry. Chill for 30 minutes.

Filling Preheat the oven to 400°F (200°C/gas 6). Combine the sugar, flour, almonds, and cinnamon in a bowl. Stir in the peaches and lemon juice. Spoon into the pie pan and dot with butter. Roll out the remaining piece of pastry and cover the filling. Brush with egg and sprinkle with raw sugar. Cut slits in the top of the pie lid to allow steam to escape during baking. Bake for 40 minutes, until golden brown. Serve warm.

SERVES 8–10 • PREPARATION 40 MIN. + $1\frac{1}{2}$ HR. TO CHILL • COOKING 40 MIN. • LEVEL 2

14 berryfruit pie

Crust
- $1\frac{1}{2}$ recipes shortcrust pastry (see page 106)

Filling
- 2 cups (300 g) fresh or frozen blueberries
- 2 cups (300 g) fresh or frozen blackberries
- 2 cups (300 g) fresh or frozen raspberries
- ½ cup (70 g) sugar
- 3 tablespoons all-purpose (plain) flour
- 1 teaspoon ground cinnamon
- ½ teaspoon ground nutmeg
- 2 teaspoons finely grated untreated lemon zest
- 1 large egg, lightly beaten
- Confectioners' (icing) sugar, to dust

Crust Prepare the shortcrust pastry. Divide into two pieces, one slightly larger than the other. Wrap in plastic wrap (cling film) and refrigerate for 1 hour. Roll out the larger piece of pastry on a floured work surface to ⅛ inch (3 mm) thick. Line the base and sides of a 9-inch (23-cm) pie pan with the pastry. Chill for 30 minutes.

Filling Preheat the oven to 400°F (200°C/gas 6). Combine all the berries, sugar, flour, cinnamon, nutmeg, and lemon zest in a bowl. Pour the filling into the pie pan. Roll out the remaining piece of pastry and cover the filling. Cut slits in the top to allow steam to escape during baking. Brush with the beaten egg. Bake for 40 minutes, until golden brown. Serve warm, dusted with confectioners' sugar.

SERVES 8–10 • PREPARATION 40 MIN. + 1½ HR. TO CHILL • COOKING 40 MIN. • LEVEL 2

15 lemon upside-down polenta cake

- 1½ cups (375 ml) water
- 1¾ cups (350 g) sugar
- 3 untreated lemons, with peel, very thinly sliced
- 1 cup (150 g) all-purpose (plain) flour
- ¾ cup (120 g) polenta (yellow cornmeal)
- ½ cup (75 g) finely ground almonds
- 1 teaspoon baking powder
- ½ cup (125 g) salted butter, softened
- 1 tablespoon finely grated untreated lemon zest
- 1 teaspoon lemon extract (essence)
- 3 large eggs
- ⅓ cup (90 ml) sour cream
- ¼ cup (60 ml) freshly squeezed lemon juice

Preheat the oven to 350°F (180°C/gas 4). Butter and flour a 9-inch (23-cm) springform pan. Stir 1¼ cups (300 ml) of water and ¾ cup (150 g) of sugar in a large frying pan over medium heat until the sugar has dissolved. Bring to a boil and simmer until the syrup begins to thicken, about 5 minutes. Add the lemons and simmer for about 8 minutes, turning once, until the lemon peel is tender. Using tongs, remove the lemon slices from the syrup and press them, overlapping, onto the bottom and sides of the prepared pan. Return the syrup to medium heat and stir in the remaining ½ cup (120 ml) of water. Simmer until the syrup is pale gold. Spoon the syrup over the lemon slices in the pan.

Stir the flour, polenta, almonds, and baking powder in a bowl. Beat the butter, remaining 1 cup (200 g) of sugar, lemon zest, and lemon extract in a bowl with an electric mixer on medium speed until pale and creamy. Add the eggs one at a time, beating until just blended after each addition. With the mixer on low speed, gradually beat in the flour mixture, alternating with the sour cream and lemon juice. Spoon into the pan.

Bake for 50–60 minutes, until a toothpick inserted into the center comes out clean. Cool the cake in the pan for 15 minutes. Loosen and remove the pan sides. Invert onto a serving dish. Serve warm.

SERVES 8–12 • PREPARATION 30 MIN. • COOKING 60–70 MIN. • LEVEL 2

16 chocolate banana cake

Cake
- 2 cups (300 g) all-purpose (plain) flour
- $\frac{1}{2}$ cup (75 g) unsweetened cocoa powder
- $1\frac{1}{2}$ teaspoons baking powder
- $\frac{1}{2}$ teaspoon baking soda (bicarbonate of soda)
- $\frac{1}{4}$ teaspoon salt
- 1 cup (200 g) sugar
- 2 large eggs
- $\frac{3}{4}$ cup (180 ml) hot water
- 1 cup (250 g) mashed ripe bananas (about 3 bananas)
- $1\frac{1}{2}$ teaspoons vanilla extract (essence)

Cream Cheese Frosting
- 3 ounces (90 g) cream cheese, softened
- $\frac{1}{4}$ cup (60 g) salted butter, softened
- 1 teaspoon vanilla extract (essence)
- 2 cups (300 g) confectioners' (icing) sugar
- $\frac{1}{4}$ cup (30 g) unsweetened cocoa powder

Cake Preheat the oven to 350°F (180°C/gas 4). Butter a 9-inch (23-cm) square baking pan. Line with parchment paper. Butter the paper. Mix the flour, cocoa, baking powder, baking soda, and salt in a large bowl. Stir in the sugar. Beat in the eggs, water, bananas, and vanilla. Spoon the batter into the prepared pan. Bake for 35–40 minutes, until a toothpick inserted into the center comes out clean. Cool the cake in the pan for 10 minutes. Turn out onto a rack. Carefully remove the paper and let cool completely.

Cream Cheese Frosting Beat the cream cheese, butter, and vanilla in a bowl until creamy. Beat in the confectioners' sugar and cocoa. Spread over the cake.

SERVES 10–12 • PREPARATION 20 MIN. • COOKING 35–40 MIN. • LEVEL 1

17 peanut butter cake

Cake
- 2 cups (300 g) all-purpose (plain) flour
- 2 teaspoons baking powder
- 6 ounces (180 g) dark chocolate, coarsely chopped
- ½ cup (125 g) salted butter, softened
- 1¾ cups (350 g) sugar
- 1 teaspoon vanilla extract (essence)
- 4 large eggs, separated
- ½ cup (125 g) smooth peanut butter
- 1 cup (250 ml) milk

Peanut Butter Frosting
- 2 cups (300 g) confectioners' (icing) sugar
- ½ cup (125 g) unsalted butter, melted
- ½ cup (125 g) smooth peanut butter

Cake Preheat the oven to 325°F (170°C/gas 3). Butter a 9-inch (23-cm) square baking pan. Mix the flour and baking powder in a bowl. Melt the chocolate in a double boiler over barely simmering water. Beat the butter, sugar, and vanilla in a bowl until creamy. Add the egg yolks one at a time. With mixer on low, beat in the chocolate, peanut butter, dry ingredients, and milk.

Beat the egg whites in a large bowl until stiff peaks form. Fold into the batter. Spoon the batter into the pan. Bake for 1¼ hours, until a toothpick inserted into the center comes out clean. Cool the cake in the pan for 10 minutes. Turn out onto a rack and let cool.

Peanut Butter Frosting Beat the confectioners' sugar, butter, and peanut butter in a bowl until smooth. Spread the top and sides of the cake with the frosting.

SERVES 12–14 • PREPARATION 30 MIN. • COOKING 1¼ HR. • LEVEL 1

18 blueberry cream cake
with cinnamon frosting

Cream Cake
- $\frac{1}{2}$ cup (100 g) superfine (caster) sugar
- 4 large eggs, separated
- $\frac{3}{4}$ cup (125 g) all-purpose (plain) flour
- 1 teaspoon ground cinnamon
- $\frac{1}{2}$ cup (125 g) salted butter, melted and cooled

Blueberry Cream Filling
- $\frac{1}{2}$ cup (125 ml) heavy (double) cream
- 2 tablespoons confectioners' (icing) sugar
- $\frac{1}{4}$ cup (60 ml) sour cream
- 1 teaspoon finely grated untreated lemon zest
- $\frac{1}{2}$ teaspoon vanilla extract (essence)
- $1\frac{1}{3}$ cups (300 g) blueberries

Cinnamon Frosting
- $1\frac{1}{3}$ cups (200 g) confectioners' (icing) sugar
- 1 teaspoon cinnamon
- 2 tablespoons boiling water

Cream Cake Preheat the oven to 350°F (180°C/gas 4). Butter a 9-inch (23-cm) round cake pan and line with parchment paper. Beat the sugar and egg yolks in a medium bowl with an electric mixer on medium speed until pale and thick. Beat the egg whites in a medium bowl with the mixer on high speed until firm peaks form. Fold a quarter of the egg whites into the yolk mixture. Add the flour and cinnamon and pour in the butter, gently folding until incorporated. Fold in the remaining whites. Spoon the batter into the prepared cake pan. Bake for 45 minutes, until golden brown and a toothpick inserted into the center comes out clean. Cool in the pan for 10 minutes. Turn out onto a rack, peel off the paper, and let cool completely.

Blueberry Cream Filling Beat the cream and confectioners' sugar in a medium bowl until soft peaks form. Beat in the sour cream, lemon zest, and vanilla. Add the blueberries, stirring until well mixed.

Cinnamon Frosting Mix the confectioners' sugar and cinnamon into a small bowl. Pour in the water, stirring until smooth and creamy.

Split the cake horizontally. Place one layer on a serving plate and spread with the blueberry and sour cream filling. Place the other half on top and drizzle with the cinnamon frosting.

SERVES 8–12 • PREPARATION 30 MIN. • COOKING 45 MIN. • LEVEL 2

19 coffee cream dacquoise

Dacquoise
- 4 large egg whites
- 1/8 teaspoon salt
- 1 cup (200 g) sugar
- 1 1/3 cups (200 g) finely ground almonds
- 1 tablespoon cornstarch (cornflour)
- 1/3 cup (50 g) confectioners' (icing) sugar, to dust
- 1/4 cup (30 g) flaked toasted almonds, to decorate

Coffee Chantilly
- 1 cup (250 ml) heavy (double) cream
- 2 tablespoons sugar
- 2 teaspoons coffee extract (essence)

Dacquoise Preheat the oven to 300°F (150°C/gas 2). Line a baking sheet with parchment paper. Mark out two 9-inch (23-cm) circles. Beat the egg whites and salt in a large bowl with an electric mixer on medium speed until frothy. Add the sugar, beating until stiff, glossy peaks form. Fold in the almonds and cornstarch. Spoon into a pastry bag fitted with a 1/2-inch (1-cm) plain tip. Pipe in spirals to fill the circles. Bake for 1 hour, until crisp. Cool for 10 minutes. Transfer to racks. Remove the paper and let cool completely.

Coffee Chantilly Beat the cream, sugar, and coffee extract until thick. Place one round of dacquoise on a serving plate. Spread with the cream. Cover with the other round. Dust with the confectioners' sugar and stick the almonds all around the sides. Refrigerate for 30 minutes before serving.

SERVES 8–10 • PREPARATION 30 MIN. + 30 MIN. TO CHILL • COOKING 1 HR. • LEVEL 2

20 orange meringue torte

Meringue Disks
- 6 large egg whites
- $1\frac{3}{4}$ cups (350 g) superfine (caster) sugar
- $2\frac{1}{2}$ cups (250 g) ground almonds
- 1 tablespoon finely grated untreated orange zest
- 2 teaspoons ground cinnamon
- 1 teaspoon ground nutmeg
- $\frac{1}{2}$ teaspoon ground cloves
- Candied (glacé) orange slices

Orange Cream
- $1\frac{1}{2}$ cups (375 ml) heavy (double) cream
- 5 tablespoons confectioners' (icing) sugar
- $\frac{1}{2}$ cup (125 ml) crème fraîche
- 1 tablespoon finely grated untreated orange zest
- $\frac{1}{2}$ teaspoon ground cinnamon
- $\frac{1}{8}$ teaspoon ground cloves

Meringue Disks Preheat the oven to 275°F (140°C/gas 1). Line a baking sheet with parchment paper. Mark out two 9-inch (23-cm) circles. Beat the egg whites in a bowl with an electric mixer on medium speed until soft peaks form. Add the sugar, beating until stiff, glossy peaks form. Fold in the almonds, orange zest, cinnamon, nutmeg, and cloves. Spoon onto the baking sheets and spread to fill the circles. Bake for 1 hour, until crisp. Cool for 10 minutes. Transfer to racks. Remove the paper and let cool completely.

Orange Cream Beat the cream and confectioners' sugar until thick. Add the crème fraîche, orange zest, cinnamon, and cloves. Spread a third of the orange cream onto each meringue disk. Place the disks one on top of the other. Arrange the candied orange slices decoratively around the outside edge of the top layer.

SERVES 8–10 • PREPARATION 30 MIN. • COOKING 1 HR. • LEVEL 2

1
cheese galettes

2
black olive crackers

3
pretzels

4
oregano breadsticks

5
bread rings

6
carrot & cumin muffins

7
ham & cheese pinwheels

8
cheese & bacon muffins

9
caramelized onion tart

10
onion quiche

11
cherry tomato quiche

12
potato & tomato quiche

13
chunky cornbread with guacamole

14
potato & Lemon loaf with rosemary

savory baking

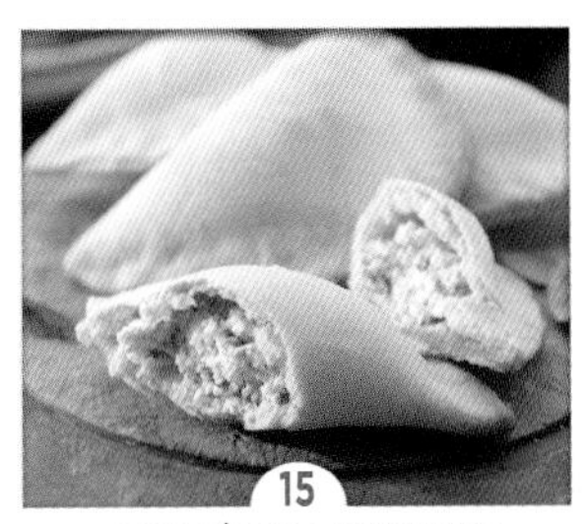
15
goat cheese turnovers

16
cheese focaccia

17
cheese & corn pull-apart

18
filled focaccia with bell peppers & gorgonzola

19
filled zucchini focaccia

20
onion & sage focaccia

1 cheese galettes

- 1 cup (250 g) salted butter, softened
- $1\frac{1}{3}$ cups (200 g) all-purpose (plain) flour
- 1 cup (120 g) freshly grated Gruyere cheese

Preheat the oven to 300°F (150°C/gas 2). Line a large baking sheet with parchment paper. Beat the butter in a bowl with an electric mixer at medium speed until smooth. Add the flour and cheese and mix at low speed until combined. Flour your hands and shape the dough into a ball. Flour the work surface and roll the dough out to ½-inch (1 cm) thick. Cut out rounds with a 2-inch (5-cm) cookie cutter. Place on the baking sheet and prick with a fork.

Bake for 8 minutes. Increase the oven temperature to 400°F (200°C/gas 6) and bake for 5–6 minutes more, until golden brown. Cool on the sheet for 5 minutes. Transfer to a rack and let cool completely.

SERVES 6–8 • PREPARATION 20 MIN. • COOKING 13–14 MIN. • LEVEL 1

2 black olive crackers

- 2 cups (300 g) all-purpose (plain) flour
- 1 teaspoon baking powder
- 1/4 teaspoon sugar
- 2/3 cup (150 g) salted butter, chilled and diced
- 1/2 cup (120 ml) milk
- 1/2 cup (70 g) freshly grated Parmesan cheese
- 1 cup (100 g) pitted black olives, finely chopped

Mix the flour, baking powder, sugar, and butter in a bowl. Add 1/3 cup (90 ml) of milk and the Parmesan. Knead into a smooth dough. Add the olives and the remaining milk, if too crumbly. Shape into a ball. Divide the ball in half. Place each half on a sheet of plastic wrap (cling film) large enough to fully enclose it. Shape into logs about 2 inches (5 cm) in diameter. Wrap and seal the ends. Place in the freezer for 45 minutes.

Preheat the oven to 350°F (180°C/gas 4). Line two baking sheets with parchment paper. Unwrap the logs of dough. Cut into 1/4-inch (5-mm) slices and transfer to the baking sheets. Bake for 10–12 minutes, until firm and golden. Cool completely on a rack.

SERVES 10–12 • PREPARATION 25 MIN. + 45 MIN. TO FREEZE • COOKING 10–12 MIN. • LEVEL 1

3 pretzels

- ½ ounce (15 g) fresh yeast or 1 (¼-ounce/7-g) package active dry yeast
- ½ teaspoon sugar
- 1 cup (250 ml) warm water
- 2 cups (300 g) all-purpose (plain) flour
- ½ teaspoon salt
- 1 large egg, lightly beaten
- 2 tablespoons coarse sea salt

Combine the yeast and sugar in a small bowl with ⅓ cup (90 ml) of water. Stir well and set aside until foamy, 5–10 minutes.

Sift the flour and salt into a large bowl. Use a wooden spoon to gradually stir in the yeast mixture. Add enough of the remaining water to make a soft dough. Transfer to a floured work surface and knead until smooth and elastic, 5–10 minutes. Shape into a ball and place in an oiled bowl. Cover with a cloth and set aside in a warm place until doubled in bulk, about 2 hours.

Preheat the oven to 450°F (225°C/gas 8). Oil two large baking sheets. Turn the dough out onto a floured work surface and divide into 12 portions. Roll each portion into a long rope and make into a pretzel shape by twisting the ends around each other. Arrange the pretzels well-spaced on the baking sheets.

Brush with the egg and sprinkle with the coarse sea salt. Bake for about 15 minutes, until golden brown. Serve warm or at room temperature.

SERVES 6–12 • PREPARATION 45 MIN. + 2 HR. TO RISE • COOKING 15 MIN. • LEVEL 2

Pretzels are made from bread dough tied in a big loose knot. Originally from central Europe, they can be sweet or savory. They make a great snack anytime of the day.

4 oregano breadsticks

- 1 recipe basic dough (see page 282)
- $\frac{1}{4}$ cup (60 g) lard (or butter), melted
- 3 tablespoons finely chopped fresh oregano or 2 teaspoons dried oregano

Prepare the dough following the instructions on page 282. Gradually work the lard and oregano into the dough as you knead. Let rise in a warm place until doubled in bulk, about $1\frac{1}{2}$ hours.

Preheat the oven to 400°F (200°C/gas 6). Oil two large baking sheets. Knead the dough briefly on a floured work surface. Break off pieces about the size of an egg and roll into logs about 12 inches (30 cm) long. Place on the prepared baking sheets, spacing well. Brush with the oil and let rise for 30 minutes.

Bake for 15–20 minutes, until crisp and golden brown. Cool on wire racks. Serve at room temperature.

MAKES 15–20 • PREPARATION 20 MIN. + 2 HR. TO RISE • COOKING 15–20 MIN. • LEVEL 2

5 bread rings

- $6\frac{2}{3}$ cups (1 kg) all-purpose (plain) flour
- 1 tablespoon salt
- $1\frac{1}{2}$ cups (375 ml) dry white wine
- 1 cup (250 ml) extra-virgin olive oil

Sift the flour and salt into a bowl. Stir in the wine and enough oil to make a firm dough. Knead on a lightly floured work surface until smooth and elastic, 15–20 minutes. Cover and let rest for 20 minutes.

Preheat the oven to 400°F (200°C/gas 6). Oil four large baking sheets. Break off pieces of dough and shape into small batons, about ½ inch (1 cm) in diameter and 3 inches (8 cm) long. Shape into rings, pinching the ends together with your fingertips.

Bring a large pot of salted water to a boil. Cook the bread rings in batches for 2–3 minutes. Remove with a slotted spoon and transfer to a clean cloth to dry. Arrange on the baking sheets. Bake for 30–40 minutes, until crisp and golden brown. Let cool on wire racks.

MAKES 70–80 • PREPARATION 45 MIN. + 20 MIN. TO REST • COOKING 50–60 MIN. • LEVEL 3

6 carrot & cumin muffins

- 2 teaspoons cumin seeds
- 2 medium carrots, about 6 ounces (180 g), coarsely grated
- 3 tablespoons pumpkin seeds
- 2 tablespoons chopped fresh cilantro (coriander)
- 1 cup (150 g) all-purpose (plain) flour
- $^{2}/_{3}$ cup (100 g) whole-wheat (wholemeal) flour
- 1 tablespoon baking powder
- 1 teaspoon baking soda (bicarbonate of soda)
- $^{1}/_{2}$ teaspoon salt
- Freshly ground black pepper
- $^{3}/_{4}$ cup (180 ml) milk
- 1 large egg, lightly beaten
- $^{1}/_{4}$ cup (60 ml) extra-virgin olive oil

Preheat the oven to 400°F (200°C/gas 6). Line the cups of a standard muffin tin with 4-inch (10-cm) squares of parchment paper.

Dry-fry the cumin seeds in a frying pan over high heat for 1–2 minutes. Place in a large bowl. Add the carrots, pumpkin seeds, and cilantro to the bowl. Add both flours, the baking powder, baking soda, salt, and pepper. Stir in the milk, egg, and olive oil. Beat with a wooden spoon until just mixed.

Divide the batter among the lined muffin cups, filling each one about two-thirds full. Bake for 20–25 minutes, until risen and firm to the touch. Cool for 5 minutes, then turn out onto a wire rack. Serve warm or at room temperature.

MAKES 10–12 • PREPARATION 15 MIN. • COOKING 20–25 MIN.
LEVEL 1

These muffins make a healthy after-school snack and are also great at brunch or with a bowl of soup at lunchtime.

7 ham & cheese pinwheels

- 1 (8-ounce/250-g) sheet ready-rolled puff pastry
- 4 ounces (120 g) thinly sliced ham
- 2 tablespoons finely chopped fresh basil
- ¾ cup (100 g) finely grated Gruyère cheese
- 1 large egg, beaten

Cut the pastry in half to make two equal rectangles. Arrange half the ham on one piece of pastry. Sprinkle with half the basil and cheese. Brush one long border with egg glaze. Starting at the long side opposite the border, roll up jelly-roll style, pressing to seal the edges. Wrap in plastic wrap (cling film). Repeat with the remaining ingredients to form a second log. Chill until firm, 3–4 hours.

Preheat the oven to 400°F (200°C/gas 6). Line two large baking sheets with parchment paper. Slice the logs into ½-inch (1-cm) thick rounds. Arrange on the sheets. Bake for 15 minutes, until golden brown. Transfer to racks and cool slightly. Serve warm.

SERVES 6–8 • PREPARATION 15 MIN. + 3–4 HR. YO CHILL • COOKING 15 MIN. • LEVEL 1

8 cheese & bacon muffins

- $2\frac{1}{3}$ cups (350 g) all-purpose (plain) flour
- $2\frac{1}{2}$ teaspoons baking powder
- 1 tablespoon sugar
- $\frac{1}{2}$ teaspoon salt
- $\frac{1}{3}$ cup (90 ml) vegetable oil
- 2 large eggs
- $1\frac{1}{4}$ cups (300 ml) milk
- 4 ounces (120 g) pancetta, finely diced
- $\frac{1}{2}$ cup (70 g) coarsely grated Cheddar + extra to sprinkle
- 4 scallions (spring onions), white part only, finely chopped

Preheat the oven to 400°F (200°C/gas 6). Line a standard 12-cup muffin tin with paper liners.

Mix the flour, baking powder, sugar, and salt in a large bowl. Whisk the oil, eggs, and milk in a bowl then stir into the flour mixture. Fold in the pancetta, cheese, and scallions. Spoon into the muffin cups.

Sprinkle with the extra grated cheese. Bake for 18–20 minutes, until risen, golden, and springy to the touch. Transfer to racks and cool slightly. Serve warm.

MAKES 12 • PREPARATION 20 MIN. • COOKING 18–20 MIN. • LEVEL 1

9 caramelized onion tart

- 1 (8-ounce/250-g) sheet ready-rolled puff pastry
- 3 slices bacon, cut into small pieces
- 1/4 cup (60 ml) honey
- 1/4 cup (60 ml) dry white wine
- 1 1/2 pounds (750 g) white onions, thinly sliced
- 3/4 cup (180 ml) crème fraîche
- 1/2 teaspoon salt
- 1/4 teaspoon freshly ground black pepper
- 1/8 teaspoon freshly grated nutmeg

Preheat the oven to 375°F (190°C/gas 5). Place the pastry on a lightly floured work surface. Fold in a 1/2 inch (1 cm) border of pastry on all sides (to stop the filling running out during baking). Put the pastry on a large baking sheet. Chill while you prepare the filling.

Fry the bacon in a small frying pan over medium heat until brown and crisp. Transfer to paper towels to drain. Reserve 1 tablespoon of bacon fat from the pan. Whisk the honey, wine, and reserved bacon fat in a large bowl. Add the onions and toss to coat.

Oil a large rimmed baking sheet. Spread the onion mixture in an even layer on the sheet. Bake, turning often, for 30–40 minutes, until caramelized.

Increase the oven temperature to 400°F (200°C/gas 6). Mix the crème fraîche, salt, pepper, and nutmeg in small bowl. Spread the crème fraîche mixture over the crust. Spread the onions on top. Sprinkle with the bacon. Bake for 20–25 minutes, until the crust is golden brown and the filling is bubbling. Serve hot.

SERVES 8–12 • PREPARATION 30 MIN. • COOKING 60–75 MIN. • LEVEL 2

10 onion quiche

- 1 (8-ounce/250-g) sheet ready-rolled puff pastry
- 12 medium white onions, thinly sliced
- 2 tablespoons extra-virgin olive oil
- 5 large eggs
- 1 cup (250 ml) heavy (double) cream
- $1^{3}/_{4}$ cups (200 g) freshly grated Emmental cheese
- Salt and freshly ground black pepper

Preheat the oven to 350°F (180°C/gas 4). Roll the pastry out on a lightly floured work surface to ⅛ inch (3 mm) thick. Line the base and sides of a 10-inch (25-cm) springform pan with the pastry.

Sauté the onions in the oil in a large frying pan over medium heat until softened, about 10 minutes. Beat the eggs, cream, and cheese in a large bowl. Season with salt and pepper. Add the onions and mix well.

Pour the onion mixture into the pastry case. Bake for 15 minutes. Increase the oven temperature to 400°F (200°C/gas 6). Bake for 15 minutes more, until golden brown and set. Serve warm or at room temperature.

SERVES 6 • PREPARATION 30 MIN. • COOKING 40 MIN. • LEVEL 2

11 cherry tomato quiche

Crust
- $1\frac{2}{3}$ cups (250 g) all-purpose (plain) flour
- $\frac{1}{2}$ cup (120 g) cold salted butter, cut up
- 2 tablespoons cold water

Filling
- 4 large eggs
- $\frac{1}{2}$ cup (120 ml) heavy (double) cream
- $\frac{1}{2}$ cup (120 g) ricotta cheese, drained
- 6 tablespoons freshly grated Parmesan cheese
- Salt and freshly ground black pepper
- 6 leaves fresh basil, finely chopped
- $\frac{1}{2}$ teaspoon dried oregano
- 15 cherry tomatoes, halved

Crust Pulse the flour, butter, and water in a food processor until just mixed. Shape into a ball, wrap in plastic wrap (cling film), and chill for 30 minutes. Preheat the oven to 350°F (180°C/gas 4). Butter a 10-inch (25-cm) springform pan.

Filling Beat the eggs, cream, ricotta, and Parmesan in a large bowl. Season with salt and pepper. Stir in the basil and oregano. Roll the pastry out to $\frac{1}{4}$ inch (5 mm) thick. Line the pan with the pastry. Pour in the egg and cheese mixture. Add the tomatoes, pressing them into the filling slightly. Bake for 45 minutes, until golden brown and set. Serve hot or at room temperature.

SERVES 6 • PREPARATION 30 MIN. + 30 MIN. TO CHILL • COOKING 45 MIN. • LEVEL 1

12 potato & tomato quiche

- 2 potatoes
- 2 large eggs
- ½ cup (120 ml) heavy (double) cream
- 1 tablespoon freshly grated Parmesan cheese
- ½ teaspoon dried oregano
- Salt and freshly ground black pepper
- 1 (8-ounce/250-g) sheet ready-rolled puff pastry
- 1 large firm-ripe tomato, thinly sliced

Preheat the oven to 400°F (200°C/gas 6). Butter an 8-inch (20-cm) springform pan or pie plate. Peel the potatoes and cut into ¼-inch (5-mm) slices. Steam the potato slices until tender, 5–10 minutes.

Beat the eggs, cream, Parmesan, and oregano in a large bowl. Season with salt and pepper.

Roll the pastry out on a lightly floured work surface to ⅛ inch (3 mm) thick. Line the prepared pan with the pastry. Arrange the potatoes and tomato on the pastry base. Pour in the egg mixture.

Bake for 15 minutes. Lower the oven temperature to 350°F (180°C/gas 4). Bake for 15 minutes more, until the pastry is golden brown and the filling has set. Serve warm or at room temperature.

SERVES 4–6 • PREPARATION 30 MIN. • COOKING 35–40 MIN. • LEVEL 1

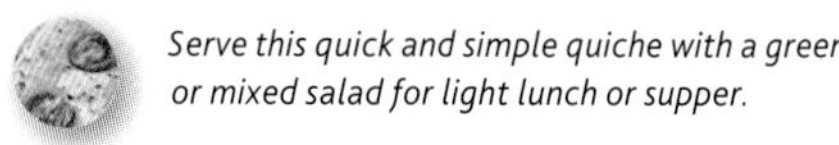

Serve this quick and simple quiche with a green or mixed salad for light lunch or supper.

13 chunky cornbread
with guacamole

Cornbread
- 1 tablespoon vegetable oil
- 1 onion, chopped
- 3 slices bacon, chopped
- 2 teaspoons cajun spice mix
- 1 cup (150 g) cornmeal (polenta)
- 1 cup (150 g) all-purpose (plain) flour
- 1 teaspoon baking powder
- ½ teaspoon salt
- 2 tablespoons sugar
- 1½ cups (375 ml) milk
- 1 large egg

Guacamole
- 1 avocado, peeled and pitted
- 1 tablespoon vegetable oil
- Freshly squeezed juice of 1 lime

Cornbread Preheat the oven to 400°F (200°C/gas 6). Grease a 9 x 5-inch (13 x 23-cm) loaf pan. Heat the oil in a large frying pan over medium heat. Add the onion and bacon and sauté until softened, 3–4 minutes. Add the cajun spice and sauté for 1 minute.

Combine the cornmeal, flour, baking powder, salt, and sugar in a large bowl. Whisk the milk and egg in a bowl until frothy. Pour into the dry ingredients and stir to combine. Stir in the bacon mixture. Pour into the pan. Bake for 20–25 minutes, until golden brown.

Guacamole Mash the avocado in a small bowl with the oil and lime juice. Serve with the cornbread.

SERVES 4–6 • PREPARATION 15 MIN. • COOKING 20–25 MIN. • LEVEL 2

14 potato & lemon loaf
with rosemary

- 2 tablespoons finely grated untreated lemon zest
- 2 tablespoons fresh rosemary
- 2 tablespoons pine nuts
- 2 cups (300 g) all-purpose (plain) flour + 1 tablespoon extra
- 2 teaspoons baking powder
- 1 cup (150 g) grated parsnip or potato
- 1 tablespoon freshly grated Parmesan cheese
- 1 cup (250 ml) buttermilk
- 1 tablespoon extra-virgin olive oil
- 2 tablespoons freshly squeezed lemon juice

Preheat oven to 375°F (190°C/gas 5). Oil a 9 x 5 inch (13 x 23-cm) loaf pan. Combine the lemon zest, rosemary, and pine nuts in a bowl. Mix the flour, baking powder, parsnip, and Parmesan in a separate bowl. Whisk the buttermilk, oil, and lemon juice in a small bowl. Pour into the flour mixture. Mix to form a soft dough. Press half the dough into the pan. Sprinkle with half the pine nut mixture. Top with the remaining dough. Mix the remaining pine nut mixture with the extra flour. Sprinkle over the loaf. Bake for 40–45 minutes, until golden brown. Serve warm.

SERVES 8 • PREPARATION 20 MIN. • COOKING 40–45 MIN. • LEVEL 1

15 goat cheese turnovers

- 1⅔ cups (250 g) all-purpose (plain) flour
- 6 tablespoons (90 ml) extra-virgin olive oil
- ⅓ cup (90 ml) water + 2 tablespoons
- 5 ounces (150 g) chèvre or other soft fresh goat cheese
- 2 tablespoons finely chopped fresh thyme
- Salt and freshly ground black pepper
- 1 large egg white

Put the flour in a large bowl. Add 3 tablespoons of oil and ⅓ cup (90 ml) water. Mix to form a smooth dough. Shape into a ball and wrap in plastic wrap (cling film). Chill in the refrigerator for 1 hour.

Stir the goat cheese in a small bowl until smooth. Add half the thyme. Season with salt and pepper.

Preheat the oven to 400°F (200°C/gas 6). Oil a large baking sheet.

Divide the dough into eight equal pieces. Roll out on a floured work surface into ⅛-inch (3-mm) thick circles. Spoon the goat cheese mixture onto one half of each circle. Beat the egg white and remaining 2 tablespoons of water in a small bowl and brush the edges of the pastry. Fold the pastry over the filling. Pinch the edges together to seal.

Transfer to the prepared baking sheet. Brush with some of the remaining oil. Bake for 5 minutes. Brush with the remaining oil. Bake until puffed and golden brown, 5–10 minutes. Serve hot.

SERVES 4–8 • PREPARATION 30 MIN. + 1 HR. TO CHILL • COOKING 10–15 MIN. • LEVEL 2

These little turnovers make a wonderful appetizer or snack. Serve them warm with a glass of chilled, fruity white wine.

16 cheese focaccia

- $3\frac{1}{2}$ cups (500 g) all-purpose (plain) flour
- 1 teaspoon salt
- $\frac{1}{4}$ cup (60 ml) + 2 tablespoons extra-virgin olive oil
- 1 cup (250 ml) water
- 12 ounces (350 g) Gorgonzola or Taleggio cheese, melted with 1 tablespoon milk
- 1 teaspoon coarse sea salt, to sprinkle

Preheat the oven to 400°F (200°C/gas 6). Oil a 9 x 13-inch (23 x 33-cm) baking pan. Mix the flour and salt in a large bowl. Stir in $\frac{1}{4}$ cup (60 ml) of oil and enough water to form a fairly soft dough. Divide in half and shape into two balls. Cover with a clean cloth and let rest for 15 minutes.

Roll both pieces of dough out to fit the pan. Place one in the pan. Cover with the cheese. Top with the other piece of dough, pressing down to seal the edges. Brush with the remaining 2 tablespoons oil of and sprinkle with the salt. Bake for 15–20 minutes until golden. Serve warm.

SERVES 6 • PREPARATION 15 MIN. + 15 MIN. TO REST • COOKING 15–20 MIN. • LEVEL 2

17 cheese & corn pull-a-part

- 1 onion, finely chopped
- 2 tablespoons extra-virgin olive oil
- 4 cups (600 g) all-purpose (plain) flour
- 1 tablespoon baking powder
- 2 teaspoons salt
- 2 cups (250 g) freshly grated Parmesan cheese + 4 tablespoons extra
- 1 (14-ounce/400-g) can corn (sweetcorn)
- 2 cups (500 ml) heavy (double) cream
- 2 tablespoons milk

Preheat the oven to 375°F (190°C/gas 5). Oil a large baking sheet. Sauté the onion in the oil in a large frying pan over medium heat until golden, 3–4 minutes.

Combine the flour, baking powder, and salt in a bowl. Stir in the Parmesan, onion, and corn. Beat the cream until stiff. Fold into the batter to form a soft dough. Turn out onto a floured work surface and knead for 1 minute. Form into a round loaf shape and place on a piece of parchment paper. Brush with the milk, then score in a checkered pattern about ⅔ inch (1.5 cm) deep. Sprinkle with the extra Parmesan. Transfer to the prepared baking sheet. Bake for 30–35 minutes, until risen and golden brown. Serve warm.

SERVES 6–8 • PREPARATION 20 MIN. • COOKING 30–35 MIN. • LEVEL 1

18 filled focaccia
with bell peppers & gorgonzola

Basic Dough
- 2 (1/4-ounce/7-g) packages active dry yeast or 1 ounce (30 g) compressed fresh yeast
- About 1 1/2 cups (350 ml) warm water
- 3 1/3 cups (500 g) all-purpose (plain) flour
- 1/2 teaspoon salt

Filling
- 1 large red bell pepper (capsicum)
- 1 large yellow pepper (capsicum)
- 1 clove garlic, thinly sliced
- 8 ounces (250 g) Gorgonzola cheese, sliced
- Freshly ground black pepper
- 4 tablespoons (60 ml) extra-virgin olive oil
- 8–10 cherry tomatoes, halved
- 1 teaspoon dried oregano

Basic Dough Place the yeast in a small bowl. Add 1/4 cup (60 ml) of warm water and stir until dissolved. Set aside until frothy, 5–10 minutes. Combine the flour and salt in a large bowl. Pour in the yeast mixture and enough of the remaining water to create a soft dough. Transfer to a floured work surface and knead until smooth and elastic, about 10 minutes. Shape into a ball and place in a clean, lightly oiled bowl. Let rise until doubled in bulk, about 1 1/2 hours.

Filling Preheat the oven to 400°F (200°C gas 6). Oil a 9 x 13-inch (23 x 33-cm) baking pan. Bake the bell peppers for 20–30 minutes, until charred all over. Put in a plastic bag and let rest for 10 minutes. Peel and seed, then slice thinly.

Turn the dough out onto a floured work surface and knead for 1 minute. Divide in two and press one piece into the prepared pan. Cover with the peppers, garlic, and cheese. Season with pepper and drizzle with 2 tablespoons of oil. Roll out the remaining dough into a rectangle large enough to cover the pan. Cover the filling with the dough. Press the cherry tomatoes into the top at regular intervals. Sprinkle with oregano and drizzle with the remaining 2 tablespoons oil. Bake for 25–30 minutes, until golden brown. Serve warm.

SERVES 6–8 • PREPARATION 45 MIN. + 1 1/2 HR. RISE • COOKING 45–60 MIN. • LEVEL 2

19 filled zucchini focaccia

- 1 recipe basic dough (see page 282)
- 2 tablespoons extra-virgin olive oil
- 2 tablespoons fresh rosemary leaves
- 3 medium zucchini (courgettes), sliced thinly lengthwise
- 8 ounces (250 g) mozzarella cheese, shredded or cut into small cubes
- Salt and freshly ground black pepper
- 1 tomato, very thinly sliced

Prepare the basic dough. Work the oil into the dough as you knead. Let rise in a warm place until doubled in bulk, about 1½ hours.

Preheat the oven to 425°F (220°C/gas 7). Preheat a grill pan or griddle over medium heat. Grill the zucchini until tender. Oil a 9 x 13-inch (23 x 33-cm) baking pan. Divide the dough in half. Press one half into the pan. Cover with the mozzarella and zucchini. Season with salt and pepper. Roll out the remaining dough until large enough to cover the pan. Place over the filling. Brush with the remaining oil. Spread the tomato on top. Sprinkle with the rosemary and salt. Bake until golden, 25–30 minutes. Serve warm.

SERVES 4–6 • PREPARATION 45 MIN. + 2 HR. RISE • COOKING 30–35 MIN. • LEVEL 2

20 onion & sage focaccia

- 1 recipe basic dough (see page 282)
- 3 large white onions, thinly sliced
- ½ teaspoon salt
- 15 leaves fresh sage
- ¼ cup (60 ml) extra-virgin olive oil

Prepare the basic dough and set aside to rise. Spread the onions out on a baking sheet, sprinkle with the salt, and let rest for 1 hour. Shake off excess salt. Oil a 9 x 13-inch (23 x 33-cm) baking pan. Spread the dough in the pan. Top with the onions and sage. Drizzle with the oil. Let rise for 30 minutes.

Preheat the oven to 400°F (200°C/gas 6). Bake until golden brown, 20–25 minutes. Serve warm.

SERVES 4–6 • PREPARATION 45 MIN. + 2 HR. RISE • COOKING 20–25 MIN. • LEVEL 2

index

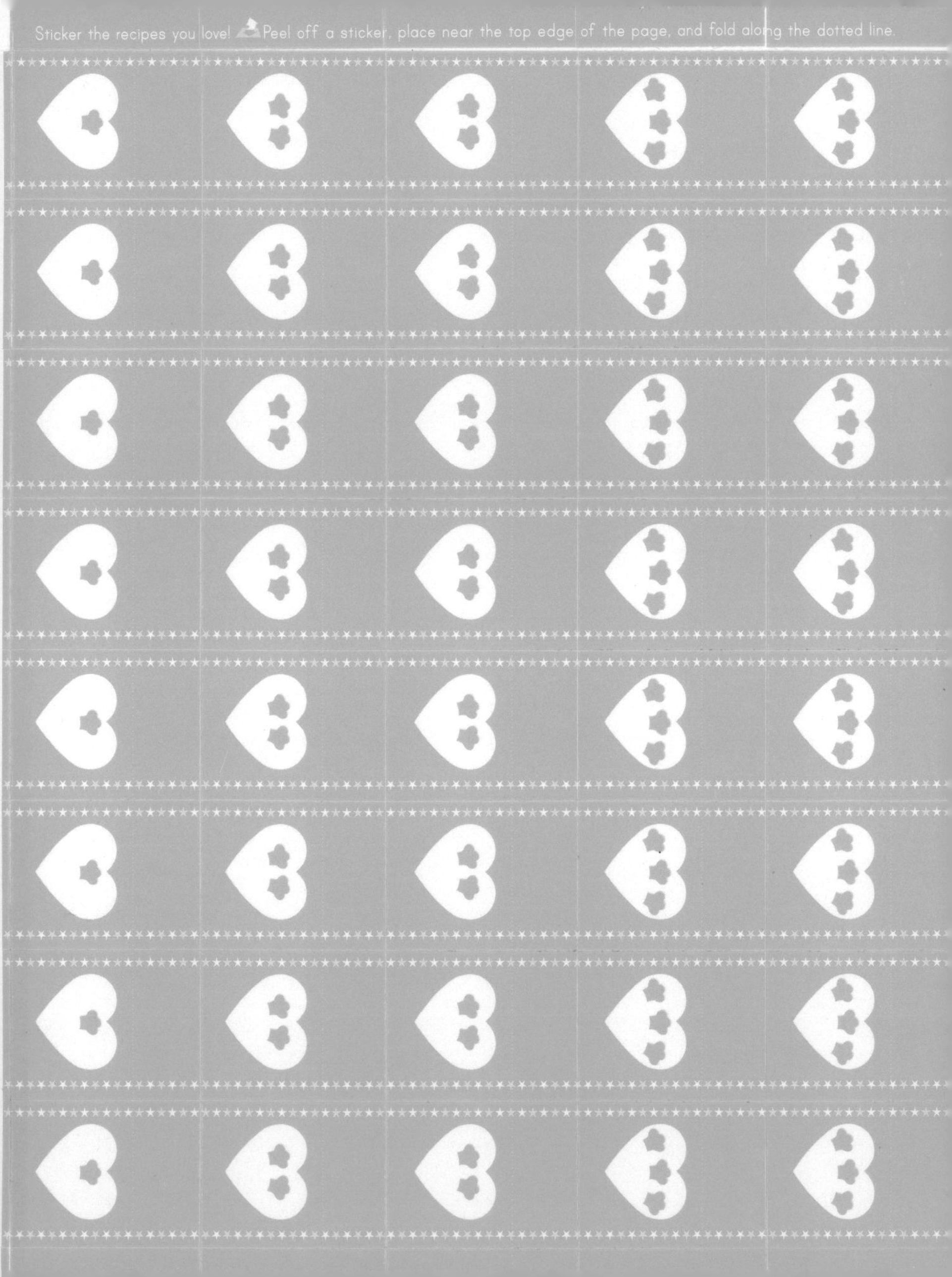
Sticker the recipes you love! Peel off a sticker, place near the top edge of the page, and fold along the dotted line.